Hannam, June, 1947-
Feminism

A Short History of a Big Idea list

Published   *Capitalism* By Peter Bowles

Feminism By June Hannam

Environmentalism By David Peterson del Mar

Communism By Mark Sandle

Available soon   *Fascism* By Martin Blinkhorn

Nationalism By Richard Bosworth

Zionism By David Engel

Terrorism By Rosemary O'Kane

Modernism By Robin Walz

Feminism

J. HANNAM

PEARSON
Longman

Harlow, England • London • New York • Boston • San Francisco • Toronto
Sydney • Tokyo • Singapore • Hong Kong • Seoul • Taipei • New Delhi
Cape Town • Madrid • Mexico City • Amsterdam • Munich • Paris • Milan

PEARSON EDUCATION LIMITED

Edinburgh Gate
Harlow CM20 2JE
United Kingdom
Tel: +44 (0)1279 623623
Fax: +44 (0)1279 431059
Website: www.pearsoned.co.uk

First edition published in Great Britain in 2007

© Pearson Education Limited 2007

The right of June Hannam to be identified as author of this work has been asserted
by her in accordance with the Copyright, Designs and Patents Act 1988.

ISBN: 978-0-582-50608-4

British Library Cataloguing in Publication Data
A CIP catalogue record for this book can be obtained from the British Library

Library of Congress Cataloging in Publication Data
Hannam, June, 1947–
    Feminism / J. Hannam.— 1st ed.
        p. cm.— (In focus)
    Includes bibliographical references and index.
    ISBN-13: 978-0-582-50608-4 (pbk.)
    ISBN-10: 0-582-50608-5 (pbk.)
  1. Feminism. 2. Feminism—History. I. Title. II. Series: In focus (Harlow,
England)

HQ1154.H25 2007
305.4209—dc22

2006046549

10 9 8 7 6 5 4
10 09 08 07

Set by 35 in 9/15pt Iowan
Printed and Bound in Malaysia (CTP-VVP)

The Publisher's policy is to use paper manufactured from sustainable forests.

Contents

Series Editor's Preface

WHAT MAKES THE WORLD MOVE? Great men? Irresistible forces? Catastrophic events?

When listening to the morning news on the radio, reading our daily newspapers, following debates on the internet, watching evening television, all of these possibilities – and more – are offered as explanations of the troubles that beset the world in the Middle East, the 'war on terror' in Iraq and Afghanistan, environmental disasters at Chernobyl or New Orleans, and genocide in Sudan or Rwanda.

Where should we look to find answers to the puzzles of the present? To psychology? To economics? To sociology? To political science? To philosophy? Each of these disciplines offer insights into the personalities and the subterranean forces that propel the events that change the world, and within each of these disciplines there are experts who dissect current affairs on the foundation of these insights.

But all of these events, these problems, and even these disciplines themselves have one thing in common: they have a history. And it is through an understanding of the history of those ideas that inspired the people behind the events, and the ideas behind the ideologies that attempted to explain and control the forces around them that we can comprehend the perplexing and confusing world of the present day.

'Short Histories of Big Ideas' aims to provide readers with clear, concise and readable explanations of those ideas that were instrumental in shaping the twentieth century and that continue to shape – and reshape – the present. Everyone who attempts to follow the events of today via newspapers, television, radio and the internet cannot help but see or hear references to 'capitalism', 'communism', 'feminism', 'environmentalism', 'nationalism', 'colonialism' and many other 'isms'. And, while most of us probably believe that we have a basic understanding of what these terms mean, we are probably much less certain about who it was that coined, invented or defined them. Even more murky is our understanding of how these concepts moved from an idea to become an ideology and, perhaps, a phenomenon that changed the world. Most bewildering may be the disputes and controversies between factions and divisions within the movements and political parties that claim to be the true followers and the legitimate heirs of those who first conceived of the concepts to which they claim to adhere.

The authors of these Short Histories have been asked to write accessible, jargon-free prose with the goal of making comprehensible to the intelligent, interested but non-expert reader these highly complicated concepts. In each instance the approach taken is chronological, as each author attempts to explain the origins of these ideas, to describe the people who created them and then to follow the twisting path they followed from conception to the present. Each author in the series is an expert in the field, with a mastery of the literature on the subject – and a desire to convey to readers the knowledge and the understanding that the research of specialist scholars has produced, but which is normally inaccessible to those not engaged in studying these subjects in an academic environment.

The work of specialists often seems remote, obscure, even pedantic, to the non-specialist, but the authors in this series are committed to the goal of bringing the insights and understanding of specialists to a wider public, to concerned citizens and general readers who wish to go beyond today's headlines and form a more comprehensive and meaningful picture of today's world.

Gordon Martel
Series Editor

Who's Who

Mary Wollstonecraft 1759-97

Her book, *Vindication of the Rights of Woman* (1792), applied ideas about the rights of man, discussed during the French Revolution, to women and emphasized the importance of education. It has been seen as a founding text of British and American feminism.

Elizabeth Cady Stanton 1815-1902

Leading figure in the early women's suffrage movement in the United States and admired internationally. She worked closely with Susan B. Antony. They founded the National Woman Suffrage Association in 1869 and produced an influential journal, *Revolution*.

Susan B. Anthony 1820-1906

A Quaker from an abolitionist background in the United States, Susan B. Anthony worked closely with Cady Stanton in campaigning for women's suffrage and women's rights. She was president of the National American Woman Suffrage Association from 1892 to 1902.

Millicent Garrett Fawcett 1847–1929

Leader of the British constitutional suffrage movement. She began campaigning for women's suffrage in the 1860s and led the National Union of Women's Suffrage Societies from 1897 to 1919.

Hubertine Auclert 1848–1914

A French suffrage campaigner who criticized many of her contemporaries for their failure to prioritise the suffrage. She had her own newspaper, *La Citoyenne* and founded a suffrage group. She was an early advocate of civil disobedience and was influenced by the militant tactics of the British suffragettes.

Anita Augspurg 1857–1943 and Lida Gustava Heymann 1868–1943

Leading members of the radical wing of the German suffrage movement. During and after the First World war they worked for peace through the Women's International League. They were forced to flee Germany in 1933.

Emmeline Pankhurst 1858–1928

The most well-known British suffrage campaigner. With her daughter Christabel she founded the Women's Social and Political Union in 1903, which pioneered militant methods. She was imprisoned on numerous occasions and inspired many others to join the movement. During the war she gave support to the war effort and formed a short-lived Women's Party in 1918.

Bertha Lutz 1894–1976

A leading campaigner for women's rights and women's suffrage in Brazil, she also attended international women's congresses during the 1920s and 30s and forged links with women from

Europe and North America. She was elected to the Chamber of Deputies in Brazil in 1936.

Sarojini Naidu 1879–1949

Played an important role in India's fight for independence and campaigned for the enfranchisement of Indian women. In 1925 she became the second woman president of the Indian National Congress.

Hudá Sha'rawi 1879–1947

A leading figure in the Egyptian feminist movement. She was active in the International Woman Suffrage Alliance in the inter-war years and her energetic advocacy of women's suffrage ensured that the issue was kept alive in Egypt during those years.

Simone de Beauvoir 1908–86

Her book, *The Second Sex* (1949), with its emphasis on woman as 'the other' and her assertion that 'one is not born, but rather becomes, a woman' influenced the ideas of 'second wave' feminism.

Betty Friedan 1921–2006

A leading figure in 'second wave feminism', Friedan published a key text, *The Feminine Mystique*, in 1963. She drew attention to the frustrations of American housewives that she labeled as the 'problem with no name'. She was one of the founders of the National Organization for Women in 1966.

bell hooks 1952–

A black American writer and social critic whose books, in particular *Ain't I a Woman?*, 1981, have been influential in providing a critique of the white, middle-class perspectives of feminism in America and Europe.

Key Dates

1760s–90s	Enlightenment debates emphasise a universal human nature and ability to reason.
1789	French Revolution – opens a space for women to take political action.
1792	Publication of Mary Wollstonecraft's *Vindication of the Rights of Woman* – founding text of British and American feminism.
1840	World Anti-Slavery Convention, London. Women's exclusion inspired American women to organize a convention for women's rights.
1848	Women's Rights Convention, Seneca Falls, United States. First meeting to focus on women's rights.
1869	Publication of John Stuart Mill's *On The Subjection of Women*. A key text linking the emancipation of women and liberal political theory that was translated into several languages.
1860s–1880s	Organizations to demand improvements in women's social and political position formed in most European countries. Beginnings of 'first wave' feminism.
1888	International Council of Women founded in Washington to foster international solidarity.
1893	Women in New Zealand are the first to gain the vote.
1903	Women's Social and Political Union founded in Britain. Became famous throughout the world for its 'militant' methods.

1904	International Woman Suffrage Alliance formed in Berlin to bring suffragists together from around the world.
1900–1914	Women's suffrage was the focus of feminist activity in Europe and North America.
1915	Women's Peace Congress at the Hague. Women's International League is formed to work for peace.
1918–22	Many countries enfranchise women in the immediate post-war period, including Austria, Canada, United States, Britain, Germany, The Netherlands, Czecho-slovakia, Sweden and the Republic of Ireland.
1920s and 30s	Struggle for women's rights and women's suffrage in Latin America, the Caribbean, Asia and parts of the Middle East. In the 1930s women gain the vote in countries such as Brazil, Uruguay, Cuba, Turkey, the Philippines, El Salvador and Puerto Rico.
1944–56	In the immediate post-war period women are enfran-chised in a variety of countries including France, Italy, Lebanon, Egypt and Ethiopia.
1949	Publication of Simone de Beauvoir's *The Second Sex* – a key text for 'second wave feminism'.
1963	Publication of Betty Friedan's *The Feminine Mystique*. Focus on women's experiences in the family which were to be central to 'second wave' feminism.
1968	Protest against Miss World contest in Atlantic City – beginnings of the Women's Liberation Movement.
1975	United Nations International Women's Year.
1976–85	United Nations Decade of Women.
1981	Greenham Peace Camp.
1980s and 90s	Backlash against feminism, in particular in the media.
1995	World Conference on Women in Beijing sponsored by the United Nations.

CHAPTER 1

Turning the world upside down

Introduction

MILLICENT FAWCETT, a leader of the British campaign for women's suffrage, claimed in 1913 that the women's movement was one of the 'biggest things that has ever taken place in the history of the world'.

Other movements towards freedom have aimed at raising the status of a comparatively small group or class. But the women's movement aims at nothing less than raising the status of an entire sex – half the human race – to lift it up to the freedom and value of womanhood. It affects more people than any former reform movement, for it spreads over the whole world. It is more deep-seated, for it enters into the home and modifies the personal character.[1]

Fawcett's words remind us of why feminism, both as an ideology and as a political practice, has been such an important and controversial issue in most countries of the world since at least the eighteenth century. At many different times and places individuals and organized groups have demanded reforms that would improve women's lives. Feminism, however, has always had the potential of doing more than that – of quite simply 'turning the world upside down'. Feminism is a cultural as well as a political movement. It changes the way women think and feel and affects how women and men live their lives and interpret the world. For this reason it has provoked lively debates and fierce antagonisms that have continued to the present day. Contemporary feminism and its concerns, therefore, are rooted in a history stretching over at least two centuries.

Starting with the late eighteenth century, this book will explore the history of feminism in a range of countries spanning several continents. The use of a broad, comparative approach will highlight the varieties of feminism and the different political and social contexts in which they developed across the world. Although feminist campaigns were usually targeted at specific governments, there was a strong international dimension to the movement as feminists sought to make links with each other across national boundaries. The development of industrial capitalism, imperialism and colonialism from the late nineteenth century onwards also ensured that women's lives would be woven together on a global scale.

Too often the priorities of white, middle-class Western women, in particular, the achievement of the vote and equal rights, are used as a lens through which to view feminism as a whole. The concerns of women in other parts of the world – for clean water, decent food and access to health care are then either marginalized or seen as somehow 'less feminist'. Comparative work draws attention to the ethnocentrism and racism of Western feminism and questions the notion of a 'universal sisterhood'. Comparisons between countries put national peculiarities to the test and highlight cross-cultural similarities and differences. They also shift the focus away from a definition of feminism that is based on an Anglo-American model (Blom 1998).

Definitions of feminism

Does 'feminism' exist? Or are the differences among feminists today so great that we should speak of 'feminisms'? In fact, such differences are nothing new; the movement has always encompassed a wide range of attitudes, concerns and strategies. A narrow focus on the contemporary movement may hide the reality that it has always been complicated – something that historians of feminism are keenly aware of. This raises the question, therefore, of what is meant by the term feminism and whether it is possible to come up with a working definition that can be applied to a variety of contexts and periods of time. Feminists themselves, and commentators on their campaigns, are bound to emphasize different issues as lying at the heart of 'modern feminism'. For some it is the demand for women's rights or the quest for female autonomy, whereas for others it is the emphasis on the common bonds uniting women in a critique of male supremacy. It is rare to find any political label that is not controversial, but to jettison labels 'would leave one without any signposts in a sea of chaos' (Caine 1997: 7).

In this book the term feminism will be used to describe a set of ideas that recognize in an explicit way that women are

---

BOX 1.1

Feminism: the defining characteristics

1 A recognition of an imbalance of power between the sexes, with women in a subordinate role to men.
2 A belief that women's condition is socially constructed and therefore can be changed.
3 An emphasis on female autonomy.

---

subordinate to men and seek to address imbalances of power between the sexes. Central to feminism is the view that women's condition is socially constructed, and therefore open to change. At its heart is the belief that women's voices should be heard – that they should represent themselves, put forward their own view of the world and achieve autonomy in their lives. This working definition is summarized in Box 1.1.

The word *féminisme*, meaning women's emancipation, was initially used in political debates in late-nineteenth-century France and the first woman to proclaim herself a *féministe* was the French women's suffrage advocate, Hubertine Auclert. Earlier in the nineteenth century it was common to refer to the 'woman movement', the 'women's movement' or to 'women's rights'. Even after 1900 when the word feminism was in more general use in Europe women might still prefer to describe themselves as suffragists rather than as feminists. In some cases, as in the United States after 1910, feminism was used by those who wanted to distinguish themselves from the 'woman movement' with its emphasis on suffrage and equal rights. The term feminism was preferred because it implied a more far-reaching revolution in relationships between the sexes, in particular, within the family. How appropriate is it, therefore, to use the word feminist when contemporaries did not describe themselves in that way? It is obviously important to take account of the language used by women themselves in specific historical periods since it helps us to understand their aims and objectives. On the other hand, the term feminist does provide a useful shorthand to convey a set of meanings that are instantly recognizable, in particular, if feminism is defined as broadly as possible. It will, therefore, be used throughout this book to refer to individual women and to social movements that challenged gender inequalities.

Women's rights, women's emancipation and women's movements

Women's rights, women's emancipation and the women's or woman movement were all used by feminists at different times and places to describe their movements and goals. These labels had complex meanings which could change over time. Women's rights campaigners demanded that women should have formal equality with men in the law, politics and in civil society. In the course of making these demands, however, some began to question whether women should simply be seeking to enter a world that was defined by men and shaped by male values. Instead they argued that women were different from men and that 'feminine' qualities should be valued in the public as well as in the private sphere. This tension between equality and difference has been present in feminist debates since the late eighteenth century and will be a persistent theme in this book.

Women's emancipation implies that broader change was needed once formal equality had been achieved. Women were unlikely to be able to take advantage of equal rights while other aspects of their social position remained the same, for example their responsibility for child care. For socialist women full emancipation could only be achieved once women were liberated from economic and class oppression. It was imperative therefore to work for the overthrow of capitalism. During the twentieth century terms such as the women's movement or women's groups took on a different meaning from the one that was common in nineteenth-century Europe. In the earlier period the women's movement was used as a term to refer to those women who acted together to challenge women's subordination. In Latin America in the 1980s and 1990s, however, the term women's movement was used to distinguish groups that made demands on behalf of the community, or who sought to uphold the status quo, from feminist movements that sought to challenge gender roles and inequalities. We need to be careful, therefore, to be clear about what particular groups and movements aimed to achieve.

Chronologies

The mid-eighteenth century is used here as the starting point for a history of feminism. In earlier centuries individual women did debate women's social position. The most well known of these are Hildegard of Bingen, founder of a vibrant convent in the twelfth century, and the fourteenth-century poet and writer, Christine de Pizan. Through their writings and actions they challenged contemporary views about a woman's place and sought greater equality for women, in particular, in education. In the period in which they were writing, however, their ideas had little impact beyond a small, educated elite. It was not until the eighteenth century that there was a marked shift in the extent and nature of the development of feminism. The number of texts dealing with women's emancipation increased and the audience for them began to grow. Women were excited by the new ideas of the Enlightenment and the upheavals of the French Revolution. They began to imagine alternative social and gender relations and came together in various forms of association to challenge male domination and to reject contemporary definitions of what it meant to be female. By the mid-nineteenth century women in Europe, North America and the white-settler colonies of Canada, New Zealand and Australia began to organize together for the first time in societies and groups whose sole purpose was to achieve changes and improvements in the social, political and economic lives of women.

This organized movement takes centre stage in most histories of feminism. The educated, articulate women who led the movement were aware that they were making history. They wanted their achievements to be recognized by future generations and to tell their own story. So they wrote autobiographies, memoirs and histories that have helped to shape the way in which we view the characteristics and aims of early feminism. This close relationship between feminist politics and the development of a history of feminism continued with the Women's Liberation Movement of the 1960s and 70s. Activists were keen to trace the origins of their movement and constructed and reconstructed their own history and traditions in line with their contemporary preoccupations. This has had important implications for the ways in which the history of organized feminism has been under-stood and for the framework within which the story has been told. Thus some ideas, individuals and campaigns have been privileged over others. The suffrage movement, in particular, has held a central place in histories of feminism, especially in Britain and the United States where it was a strong and highly visible campaign. A focus on suffrage, however, can be a distorting lens through which to view feminism as a whole. Many women had other priorities, in particular, if they were involved in nationalist, anti-colonial and revolutionary struggles, and we need to make sure that their attempts to pursue women's social, economic and political rights are not lost from view.

A focus on well-organized women's movements has led to the development of a common narrative in histories of feminism that identifies two key periods of activism – 'first wave' feminism, c. 1860s to 1920 and 'second wave' feminism in the 1960s and 70s. This has been adapted slightly to fit the context of some other European countries. In Denmark, for example, three waves have been identified. The first in the late nineteenth century, before demands were made for the suffrage, the second, suffrage phase, just before and during the First World War and the third wave in the 1970s. In Norway there was a long first wave, going up to the end of World War Two and then a second wave from the 1960s to the 1980s, but with two 'crests' in the 1880s and 1970s. The use of waves as a metaphor can, however, be problematic. A focus on 'ebbs and flows' draws attention away from continuities and lines of tradition and reinforces the assumption that in periods of 'ebb' little feminist activity took place. This means that we can miss the variety of ways in which feminists continued to press for change in a hostile political climate, for example in the inter-war years (Legates 2001: 282). The 'two wave' model, drawn from the experiences of Britain and the United States, provides a chronological framework that is misleading when applied to other countries. It assumes that the main gains for women's suffrage had been won by 1920, after which the movement fragmented, and yet in South America the inter-war years proved far more significant, while in the 1940s over half the female population of the world still did not have the vote.

These are important reminders that we need to take care that the metaphors that we use, such as 'waves', illuminate rather than constrain our understanding of feminist activities. Thus women's attempts to challenge aspects of their social role in 'quieter' periods need to be rescued from obscurity and seen as a key part of the history of feminism. At the same time we should not underestimate the impact of high-profile, public campaigns which raised 'feminist consciousness' in an explicit way. The suffrage campaign and the Women's Liberation Movement, for instance, generated widespread publicity, influenced contemporary politics and affected the ways in which women and men thought about themselves and their place in the world. Historians have therefore searched for other ways to describe 'phases' in feminist history that can differentiate between periods of intense activity, while at the same time not ignoring that there were continuities in feminist campaigns or privileging one chronological framework over another.

An important and influential American historian of feminism, Karen Offen, prefers a metaphor derived from the study of volcanoes. Her comparative study of European feminisms has led her to suggest that feminism is a 'rather fluid form of discontent that repeatedly presses against . . . weak spots in the sedimented layers of a patriarchal crust', with the task of the historian, like that of the geologist, to 'map and measure the terrain, to locate the fissures, to analyse the context in which they open . . . and to evaluate the shifting patterns of activity over time' (2000: 25–6). A senior scholar with the Institute for research on Women and Gender at Stanford University, Offen is also a founder and past secretary-treasurer of the International Federation for Research in Women's History. Her comparative work raises many issues that are explored in the course of this book.

Themes

In a book of this size it is not possible to provide a detailed account of the development of feminism in individual countries. Emphasis is placed, therefore, on identifying broad trends and changes over time and on introducing recent interpretations and approaches. There are a number of key themes. Firstly, the challenge made by feminists to prevailing ideas about a 'woman's place'. From the late eighteenth century onwards it was assumed that there was a separation between public and private space. Women's identification with the family and domesticity, or the private sphere, was then used to justify their exclusion from the public world of work and politics. For feminists it was important to contest these ideas and to dispute their exclusion from public life, in particular from the exercise of citizenship. In doing so they challenged contemporary definitions of masculinity and femininity, re-defined what it meant to be female, and used imagination to look forward to a society in which gender relations would be transformed (Yeo 1997: Introduction).

Feminists did not develop their ideas in a vacuum but had to engage with an existing framework of social and political thought – this in turn helped to shape the characteristics of feminism at different times and places. The complex relationship between equality and difference, a second theme in the book, provides a good example. Feminists did not necessarily challenge the view that women had different qualities and characteristics from men, but used this to their own advantage. They argued that because women were different then they needed to exert an influence for good in the world beyond the family and so they needed equal rights in politics, employment and the law. There could be tensions, however, in bringing these perspectives together and also between the demand for personal autonomy and collective responsibility towards others. These tensions were then worked out in different ways by individual feminists and by the movements of which they were a part.

A further theme will focus on sisterhood. Feminists attempted to develop a politics based on women's solidarity with each other at both a national and at an international level. 'Sisterhood is powerful' was one of the key slogans of the Women's Liberation Movement of the 1960s and 70s. And yet differences of class, race, nation and sexual orientation constantly threatened to undermine this solidarity. Separate women's organizations played a key role in developing a sense of collective identity and a 'feminist consciousness', but did not provide the only space in which women could make their demands. Many feminists sought to achieve their goals through mixed-sex political parties and viewed their feminist causes as inextricably linked to a broader political agenda. Thus, they had to juggle competing loyalties and political identities, often making difficult choices over the course of a lifetime. Some feminists prioritized gender issues throughout their lives, while others shifted the focus of their political interests over time, in some periods prioritizing the fight against racism or class exploitation rather than women's subordination to men. Therefore, the relationship between feminism and other social and political reform movements, including nationalist struggles, socialist politics and anti-colonial movements will form a major theme for this study.

Feminist ideas, in theory and in practice, were complex. It is important, therefore, not to be too quick to label individuals as feminist or non-feminist on the basis of an ideal model of what a feminist should look like. Women expressed a variety of ideas, and took many different routes, as they tried to challenge inequalities in their lives. Whether they worked in single-sex groups or in mixed-sex political parties feminists had to develop effective tactics. This meant making compromises and negotiating with others who had a different agenda. What they had in common, however, was a vision of a different world for women in which they could imagine possibilities that were not confined by rigid sex roles. To achieve this world they were ready to risk imprisonment, ill health and public ridicule. As Josephine Butler, leader of the British campaign to repeal the Contagious Diseases Acts, wrote in 1871: 'English women will be found ready again and again to agitate, to give men no repose, to turn the world upside down if need be, until impurity and injustice are expelled from our laws.'[2]

Further reading

A key text that provides a detailed and thought provoking comparison of feminist ideas and movements in a wide range of

European countries is Karen Offen, *European Feminisms, 1700–1950: A Political History*, Stanford, CA: Stanford University Press, 2000. Other comparative studies of Europe include: Gisela Bock, *Women in European History*, Oxford: Blackwell, 2002; and Barbara Caine and Glenda Sluga, *Gendering European History*, London: Leicester University Press, 2000.

Europe and North America are compared in Marlene Legates *In Their Time. A History of Feminism in Western Society*, London: Routledge, 2001.

For a comparative study that not only looks at Europe, North America and Australia, but also goes further afield to include Japan, Argentina, Chile, Colombia and Uruguay, see Caroline Daley and Melanie Nolan (eds) *Suffrage and Beyond: International Feminist Perspectives*, Auckland: Auckland University Press, 1994. This was a pioneering study that drew attention to the extent to which the history of feminism had been viewed through the perspective of a model drawn from Britain and North America.

The complex relationship between feminism and nationalism is explored in: Richard J. Evans, *The Feminists: Women's Emancipation Movements in Europe, America and Australasia, 1840–1920*, London: Croom Helm, 1977; and Mrinalini Sinha, Donna J. Guy and Angela Woollacott (eds) Special Issue on Feminisms and Internationalism, *Gender and History*, 10, 3, 1998. Kumari Jayawardena examines feminism and nationalism in 12 countries in Asia and the Middle East in *Feminism and Nationalism in the Third World*, London: Zed Books, 1986.

Studies of Western feminist involvement in the project of imperialism and colonialism reveal the multiple ways in which the local, the national and the global intersect. They also draw attention to the ethnocentrism and racism of Western feminism.

See, for example, Ian C. Fletcher, Laura E. Nym Mayhall and Philippa Levine (eds) *Women's Suffrage in the British Empire: Citizenship, Nation and Race*, London: Routledge, 2002; Antoinette Burton, *Burdens of History: British Feminists, Indian Women and Imperial Power, 1865–1914*, Chapel Hill, NC: University of North Carolina Press, 1994; and Catherine Hall, Keith Mclelland and Jane Rendall (eds) *Defining the Victorian Nation: Class, Race, Gender and the Reform Act of 1867*, Cambridge: Cambridge University Press, 2000.

The comparative texts referred to above all discuss different definitions of feminism. In addition, Barbara Caine suggests that women's rights were at the core of modern feminism in *English Feminism, 1780–1980*, Oxford: Oxford University Press, 1997. Jane Rendall also employs the term modern feminism to describe the late eighteenth century onwards and uses the word feminist 'to describe women who claimed for themselves the right to define their own place in society, and a few men who sympathised with them': Jane Rendall, *The Origins of Modern Feminism: Women in Britain, France and the United States, 1780–1860*, Houndmills: Macmillan, 1985, pp. 1–2. For an argument that feminism can be used to describe periods when it was not employed by contemporaries, see Barbara Taylor, *Eve and the New Jerusalem. Socialism and Feminism in the Nineteenth Century*, London: Virago, 1983. The opposite position is explored in Nancy Cott, *The Grounding of Modern Feminism*, New Haven, CT: Yale University Press, 1986.

Women's critique of their subordinate position before the late eighteenth century is explored in Gerda Lerner, *The Creation of Feminist Consciousness: From the Middle Ages to 1870*, Oxford: Oxford University Press, 1993.

The use of the term 'waves' in histories of feminism is discussed in: Karen Offen (2000); Drude Dahlerup, 'Three Waves of Feminism in Denmark'; and Beatrice Halsaa, 'The History of the Women's Movement in Norway' – both in Gabriele Griffin and Rosi Braidotti (eds) *Thinking Differently: A Reader in European Women's Studies*, London: Zed Books, 2002.

Notes

1 M. Fawcett, 'Introduction' in H.M. Swanwick, *The Future of the Women's Movement*. London, G. Bell, 1913, p. xii quoted in K. Offen, *European Feminisms, 1700–1950: A Political History*. Stanford, CA: Stanford University Press, 2000, p. 2.

2 Quoted in A. Summers, *Female Lives, Moral States*. Newbury: Threshold Press, 2000, p. 126.

CHAPTER 2

The beginnings of modern feminism

Introduction

WHEN AND WHERE DID MODERN FEMINISM BEGIN?
What did feminists hope to achieve? Did they see themselves as
feminists? It was not until the middle of the nineteenth century
that women began to organize themselves into groups with the
purpose of challenging their subordinate position and achieving
improvements in their lives. They faced a formidable task since
legal barriers, religious beliefs, economic interests and political
systems all stood in their way. Nevertheless, some women in
western Europe and North America began from the late eighteenth century to demand that their voices be heard.

The Enlightenment and the
French Revolution

The ferment of new ideas, political upheavals and economic
change in late eighteenth-century Europe provided the perfect

---

BOX 2.1

The Enlightenment

A series of philosophical and political debates in the eighteenth century. Common characteristics include:

- a secular critique of institutions such as the monarchy and the established church;
- arguments for change based on historical, sociological and scientific premises rather than on theology;
- optimism about the potential of human reason for a fuller understanding of the natural world.

To achieve this potential individuals needed freedom of speech and of religion along with a political voice so that they could reshape the political order on the basis of the natural world. This challenged the continuation of political structures that were inherited from the past and linked to monarchical constraints and privileges.

---

conditions for feminist ideas to develop. Gender issues were at the heart of contemporary debates known as the Enlightenment (Box 2.1).

Political thinkers and philosophers who took the lead in developing Enlightenment thought emphasized the importance of a universal human nature and the ability to reason. Universality, however, did not seem to encompass women since most writers claimed that there were physical and intellectual differences between the sexes. Medical and scientific opinion was used to support the view that social and cultural differences were natural, or biologically based, rather than socially constructed. Men were thought to be rational, objective and scientific in their thinking, whereas women were seen as emotional, sensual, lacking in innate reason and a barrier to social progress. These different characteristics were used as the basis for definitions of masculinity and femininity well into the nineteenth century and beyond.

They did not, however, go unchallenged. Women expressed alternative views on marriage, education and politics in an out-pouring of novels, articles and pamphlets from the mid-eighteenth century. In salons in France or in literary circles in England small groups of well-educated women began to meet together in an attempt to influence intellectual and cultural life. They drew a response from the French writer Jean Jacques Rousseau whose influential text on education, *Emile* (1762), explored the socio-political implications of sexual difference. For him, boys needed education to develop their natural instincts for independence, autonomy and freedom which in turn suited them for public life and citizenship. In contrast, education for women should be designed to fit them for a domestic role where they could concentrate on motherhood and act as 'the carriers . . . of a new morality through which the un-naturalness of civilisation . . . could be transcended' (Outram 1995: 84). Within this domestic space women were to be subordinate legally and politically to their husbands.

The French Revolution of 1789 added a new dimension to these debates. It raised the question of what it meant to be an active citizen in the new republic and opened a space for women to take political action. When Tom Paine epitomized the ideals of the Revolution in his famous text, *The Rights of Man*, women demanded that they too should be included. And yet when the revolutionaries drew up their first constitution a distinction ·

was drawn between active citizens, who were property-owning males over the age of 21, and passive citizens, such as women and domestic servants. Political activists and commentators were quick to challenge this definition. The monarchist Olympe de Gouges, for example, in her book, *Les Droits de la Femme* (1791), called for women to enjoy equality with men in the public sphere. She accepted that men and women had different social roles but thought that this was a strength rather than a weakness. She argued that women would play a more conciliatory role in the Assembly and that this would be good for the nation.

The influence of Mary Wollstonecraft

Mary Wollstonecraft's book, *A Vindication of the Rights of Woman* (1792) was the most influential text written by a woman to come out of the French Revolution.

Wollstonecraft and her circle of radical intellectual friends welcomed the French Revolution and were influenced by the ideas expressed about the 'rights of man'. She argued that women were just as capable as men of exercising reason and virtue but had been encouraged to see themselves as governed by their feelings and as existing only to please a man. In her view, women needed education to develop their character and to enable them to contribute to shaping the new social order. In common with many other writers of the time Wollstonecraft also believed that equal intellectual capabilities could sit side by side with different social roles. She suggested, therefore, that women's sphere of expertise was motherhood and that the raising of children could contribute to the development of the republic.

BOX 2.2

Mary Wollstonecraft (1759–97)

Mary Wollstonecraft's book, A Vindication of the Rights of Woman (1792) is considered to be the founding text of British and American feminism. Born in London, she worked as a writer, translator and critic for the publisher Joseph Johnson who introduced her to an influential group of radical thinkers including Tom Paine, author of Rights of Man (1791–2), and her future husband William Godwin. Along with other members of this circle Wollstonecraft was deeply influenced by the French Revolution and the ideas expressed in the Declaration of the Rights of Man. In A Vindication she applied these ideas to women, arguing that if women were given the same educational opportunities as men they would become enlightened citizens, rational mothers and, if single, more able to find employment.

Wollstonecraft also produced two novels and a number of political and educational texts. Her private life challenged conventional morality (she lived with Gilbert Imlay outside marriage and bore him an illegitimate daughter) – this meant that her ideas were looked on with some suspicion by the nineteenth-century women's movement. Her reputation was partly rehabilitated, however, when Millicent Fawcett, leader of the British suffrage movement, wrote a sympathetic preface to a new edition of A Vindication in 1891. Mary married Godwin in 1897 but died in childbirth in the same year.

Mary Wollstonecraft's powerful message, that a change in women's 'character' and outlook would transform the social order for everyone, inspired many nineteenth-century feminists in Britain. But her republican politics and unconventional private life meant that her influence was rarely acknowledged at the time. It was not until the twentieth century that her influence on feminist ideas and on the women's movement was given greater recognition.

The explicit exclusion of women from active citizenship during the French Revolution encouraged them to make demands on behalf of their sex. They established their own organizations to call for government support for educational and social work and also for women's complete equality with men. These activities aroused so many suspicions that in 1793 women were banished from public life. They no longer had the right to attend meetings or to parade in the streets and this was later reinforced when Napoleon came to power. And yet the revolutionaries did see women as having a key part to play in developing the new republic. Through their role as 'patriotic mothers' they would educate their children into the values of republican citizenship. This emphasis on mother educators might seem to give a boost to the notion that women should be identified largely with home and family, but it also gave women an innovative and semi-public role. The notion of 'patriotic motherhood', which was also a feature of nationalist movements in the nineteenth century, could then be used by feminists to promote women's education and to demand equal access to the public sphere.

Separate spheres

In the short term, however, legal, economic and social changes reinforced women's identification with domesticity. Their subordination to men within marriage and the family was at the heart of the Napoleonic Code, introduced in 1804 (see Box 2.3).

BOX 2.3

Napoleonic Code 1804

The Code gave a husband full legal powers over his wife, her property and her children and there were harsh penalties if she committed adultery. The Code was widely adopted by other countries in Europe, either as a result of their being conquered by Napoleonic armies or through choice, and included Italy, Belgium, Holland and the German states. The Habsburg Empire borrowed from some aspects of the Code, while Britain had its own framework of laws giving men ownership of their wives' person, property and earnings and denying women most rights over their children.

Rapid urbanization and industrialization also led to an emphasis on women's domestic role, although the pace and timing of this varied in different countries. Waged work increasingly took place away from the family and became identified with men and masculinity. This had the dual effect of ensuring that women's paid employment was seen as marginal, thereby justifying low pay, and reinforcing the view that women's natural role was in the home. Working-class women still needed to contribute to family income, but their right to employment was challenged as men sought to achieve a 'family wage'. For the middle class, who were growing in wealth and influence during these years, the withdrawal of women from making an active contribution to family income was seen as a mark of status and was integral to the way in which they developed a class identity. Even if middle-class women needed, or wanted, paid employment they found that they were hampered by their lack of education and were excluded from most professions. An ideology

BOX 2.4

Separate spheres

A term used to describe the different social roles expected of
men and women in the nineteenth century. It was assumed that
biological and social differences between the sexes affected
both their personalities and their suitability for particular tasks.
Thus, men were seen as rational, aggressive and competitive, and
therefore fitted for the world of work and public activity, whereas
women were emotional, nurturing and passive, and therefore
most suited to look after the family within a domestic setting.
According to medical and religious writings, these characteristics,
and the separate male and female spheres that arose from them,
were 'natural' and ordained by God. These ideas underpinned
republican and liberal political theories and were used to justify
women's economic and legal dependence on men.

The concept of separate spheres, however, did not necessarily
reflect the reality of women's lives since it was employed in
complex and contradictory ways and could be affected by class,
religion and nationality. Members of the women's movement
used it to their own advantage in claiming a place for women
in public life on the basis of the different qualities that they
could bring.

of domesticity, therefore, based on the concept of a separation of
spheres between the sexes, came to dominate political and social
thought during the first half of the nineteenth century.

In practice, of course, women were not entirely constrained by
the private world of the family. There was no hard and fast divid-
ing line between the public and the private. The home itself can
be seen as a 'political space' since it was the 'the site of salons,
informal discussion groups, political correspondences, ideologic-
ally motivated consumer choices . . . all of which were crucial to

the emergence of specific radical political cultures' (Gleadle 2001: 151). Women active in the anti-slavery movement in Britain and America met in each others' homes, made articles for sale at bazaars and boycotted goods produced using slave labour. Such activities remind us that women could be inspired by contemporary definitions of femininity, in particular, their caring and moral qualities, to attempt to make a difference in the world. Therefore, they joined temperance and philanthropic organizations as well as contributing to the campaign against slavery.

Early nineteenth-century social and political reform movements

Did involvement in social, political and moral reform movements lead to an interest in women's rights? Some women were far more concerned with moral and religious questions than with gender inequalities, while others might be just too busy to get involved with women's rights. The British Unitarian Mary Carpenter, for example, a leading social reformer, was willing to speak in favour of women's suffrage, but gave most of her energies to the cause of destitute children. Nonetheless, many of the women who were inspired to work with her also became convinced that the vote was necessary so that they could influence social legislation and went on to play an active part in the women's movement. This complex relationship is also mirrored in the anti-slavery campaign. In Britain, a commitment to anti-slavery work delayed women's involvement in feminist politics until the cause had been won. But women did gain experience of working together, corresponded with each other across the Atlantic and developed friendship networks

they could draw on in developing an organized women's movement (Midgley 1992: 174).

Involvement in the anti-slavery campaign also encouraged
women to question aspects of their own social position. They
drew an analogy between the position of slaves on plantations
and their own sexual, legal, emotional and physical slavery to
men within marriage. This could then inspire them to make
demands on behalf of their sex, whether at home or in European colonies. Feminists continued to draw on the metaphor
of slavery to describe their own position in the late nineteenth
and early twentieth centuries. They felt able to identify, as
women, with the sufferings of others, including those in countries subject to colonial rule, and used this in making a claim for
political rights (Burton 2002: 19).

Utopian socialism, radicalism and revolution

Utopian socialists added a further dimension to the debates
around women's emancipation in the 1820s and 30s. Charles
Fourier and Saint-Simon, political theorists from France, both
envisaged a new communal society that would be free from all
inequalities, including sex inequality. They were committed to
a general movement for 'human liberation' that would include
changes in women's social position. Indeed, Fourier argued
that the degree to which women were emancipated provided a
measure of how far general emancipation had been achieved.
Socialists wanted to put their ideas into practice and formed
communities in France, Britain and the United States. These
sought a transformation in all areas of life, including marriage
and the organization of the household, rather than focusing

exclusively on new forms of production. Women took an active part as speakers and as members of the communities. The most well known female propagandist was the French socialist, Flora Tristan, who argued in her writings and speeches to working men that the emancipation of women and of workers was inextricably linked. In Britain, where the movement was associated with the cotton manufacturer Robert Owen, many female propagandists came from working-class backgrounds, including Eliza Macauley and Frances Morrison, while in France the Saint Simonians Suzanne Voilquin, Désirée Gay and Jeanne Deroin were all young, working women. Although Utopian socialism declined in the 1840s, the links made between the emancipation of women and of workers were to re-surface during the socialist revival of the late nineteenth century. In Britain a number of women influenced by Owenite socialism took their radical views and unconventional behaviour with them into the feminist campaigns of the 1850s and 60s.

Socialist women also took part in the revolutions of 1848 in Europe that challenged conservative regimes and sought to achieve representative governments and a range of civil liberties. In the process women again raised their own demands. In France Jeanne Deroin called for women's participation in public affairs and argued that only with the end of male privileges in politics could a new society be achieved. She disseminated her views through her own journal, *La Voix des Femmes*. After declaring that she would stand as a candidate for office she was arrested, with Pauline Roland, and imprisoned for trying to organize male and female workers. Using arguments that were common in the French Revolution, Deroin claimed that women, as 'humanitarian mothers', needed a political voice to safeguard the future of their children and to show men how to achieve harmony. In a slightly different vein, Louise Otto, a single, well-educated woman from an upper-middle-class background, insisted that women could make a distinctive contribution to the building of a German nation. For Otto, womanly qualities included courage, patriotism and the desire for peace and morality. However, if they were to develop their 'true womanliness' to the full women needed education and economic independence.

In Britain women formed female associations to support Chartism, a working-class movement that called in 1838 for all men to have the vote. When Chartism declined in the early 1850s, supporters in Sheffield set up a suffrage society to demand votes for women. They were influenced by the radical Quaker, Anne Knight, an anti-slavery campaigner, who wrote one of the first pamphlets calling for women's suffrage. She had connections with outspoken abolitionists in the United States, including Lucretia Mott and Elizabeth Cady Stanton who had been incensed by their exclusion from the World Anti-Slavery Convention held in London in 1840. As a result they were determined to hold a convention on women's rights when they returned home. This was finally held at Seneca Falls, New York, in 1848 – a key event in the history of organized feminism. Three hundred delegates passed resolutions on married women's rights, divorce and the need for employment and educational opportunities. Stanton's reso-lution that it was women's duty to secure the franchise was the most controversial, but it was accepted with a narrow majority.

The demand for women's emancipation developed as part of a much broader radical campaign – to free slaves, to introduce representative government, to advance the rights of workers and to achieve property reforms. Links were already being made between like-minded women in different countries. In 1851, for example, Jeanne Deroin and Pauline Roland wrote from their prison in France to the Second National Women's Convention held in the United States, sending greetings to their sisters of America and Great Britain who were united with them 'in the vindication of the right of woman to civil and political equality' (Rendall 1985: 320). In the political upheavals of the period women from all social classes found a space to articulate their own demands. They challenged the legal, political and economic constraints on their lives, but also used notions of difference to support their demands for a public role.

Did the mid-nineteenth-century women's movement arise from a reaction against the restrictions placed on women, in particular unmarried middle-class women who needed to gain employment? Or did it arise from an attempt by women to extend a public role that was already enjoyed by many? The answer is a complex one lying somewhere between these two positions. As already noted, women were involved in a range of social and political reform movements and organizations which gave them political skills and established a network of contacts. But the restrictions that they experienced, along with the belief that they should use their female values for the good of the community, also provided an impetus towards involvement in feminist politics.

The organized women's movement in the mid-nineteenth century

The precedent set by the United States was soon followed in Europe. The first women to establish organizations to demand their rights and to gain improvements in their social position were to be found in Britain, France and Germany, but these were followed swiftly after 1870 by Italy, Belgium, The Netherlands and Scandinavia. Well-educated, middle-class women predominated in these organizations, although the term 'middle-class' covered a wide range of backgrounds. The unmarried daughters of low-income clergymen worked together with the wives of wealthy industrialists and with women in professional employment such as school teaching or medicine. Men, in particular the relatives of women activists, often gave practical and emotional support. In France, for example, the republican journalist Leon Richer established a newspaper, *Le Droit des Femmes* (1869) to campaign for women's legal rights and approximately 50% of the members of French feminist groups were male. Individual working-class women did take part in the movement and gained a reputation for their propaganda skills but their numbers remained small. After the political upheavals of 1848 there was a conservative backlash against radical, feminist and socialist politics. This made it difficult to sustain the 'challenging and subversive' side of feminism (Taylor 1983: xvii). The leaders of the women's movement were anxious to emphasize the moderation and respectability of their movement and to distance themselves from political and sexual radicalism.

In the mid-nineteenth century single, middle-class women were in a difficult position if they had no male relatives support them. Their education did not prepare them for employment and they were hampered by legal and other restrictions. Thus, key demands of the women's movement at this stage were the provision of secondary and higher education for women and access to professional employment. Women's suffrage was also highlighted in Britain and the United States but was seen as a more controversial demand in France and Germany. Here it was feared that support for suffrage might harm other causes. Feminists were not, however, just narrowly focused on equal rights. They also took an interest in the family and in moral issues, including the legal position of married women, marital violence and the double standard of morality between the sexes. The regulation of prostitution by the state came in for particular criticism (see Box 2.4). Feminists in Britain, France, Germany and Finland argued that such regulation sanctioned vice and gave men even more control over women's bodies. They sought to reinforce

---

BOX 2.5

The Contagious Diseases Acts

In the context of concern about the spread of venereal disease in the armed forces a series of Acts were passed in Britain in the 1860s, known as the Contagious Diseases Acts.

The Acts applied to garrison towns and gave the police and magistrates the power to arrest any woman suspected of being a prostitute. She was then medically examined to determine whether she was suffering from a venereal disease and could be sent to a Lock hospital for up to nine months for treatment. The Acts only applied to prostitutes and not to their male clients.

A number of groups were formed to campaign for the repeal of the Acts, including the Ladies National Association (LNA) led by Josephine Butler. An all-female group, the LNA added a feminist dimension to the campaign by criticizing the power that the Acts gave to men to control women's bodies and highlighting the double standard of morality between the sexes. The Acts were suspended in 1883 and finally repealed in 1886, although they still applied in India and other British colonies.

---

the view that sexual relations should take place within marriage and criticized the double standard inherent in the belief that men were less able than women to curb their sexual desires.

Feminists were often divided in their views about prostitution, pornography and other aspects of sexual behaviour. In Britain, for example, some feminists began to look to the state to play a positive role in protecting young girls from sexual abuse and in reducing prostitution. They joined social purity groups in the late nineteenth century but their feminist views often became lost in a general attack on vice in which women were seen as victims.

The women's movement in different countries shared many goals and characteristics in common, but there were also national differences. In the United States native born women of rural New England predominated and they used the language of the Declaration of Independence to claim individual, natural rights, including the suffrage. Inspired by the view that it was women's special mission to undertake moral reforms they were very active in temperance, social reform and anti-slavery movements. Similarly in Britain women were extensively involved in philanthropic work, but feminists were largely drawn from urban industrial and professional families who were rooted in a dissenting reform tradition. Aware of class differences, they took an interest in industrial reform and the position of working-class women as well as a range of equal rights campaigns, including women's suffrage. In Catholic France there was far less opportunity for women to organize together for philanthropic purposes and there was 'no easy route to humanitarian and political activity, such as the anti-slavery or anti Corn Law movements in Britain' (Rendall 1985: 299). The women's movement was far weaker in terms of support and was to become a moderate, bourgeois movement linked with republicanism. Emphasis was placed on educational and legal reforms rather than the franchise since Republicans feared that women would use their votes to support the monarchy and the church.

Women met regularly in small groups to discuss ideas and to give each other support. Sometimes, as in Britain, there were separate committees to campaign for specific issues such as the expansion of secondary education or the repeal of the Contagious Diseases Acts. At others, for instance in France and Germany, there were general associations that took up a range of causes. Tactics included lobbying politicians, gathering signatures for petitions and publicizing ideas through public meetings, pamphlets and newspapers. It was a radical and courageous act for women to address an audience outside the home since their appearance in a public space was equated with immorality. Public meetings were most common, therefore, in the 'liberal' societies of Britain and the United States.

Feminists also published their own journals. Amongst the most well known were the *Englishwoman's Journal* (1858) and *The Revolution*, founded in the United States in 1868 by Elizabeth Cady Stanton and Susan B. Anthony. But nearly every country had its own publication including the Spanish Journal *La Voz de la Mujer* (Woman's Voice), *Nylaende* (New Frontiers) published in Norway in 1887 and *La Donna*, which appeared in Italy between 1868 and 1892. The importance of these journals cannot be overstated. They provided a space for feminists to challenge prevailing ideas about appropriate social roles for women and brought like-minded women in touch with each other.

Liberal democracies provided the most fertile ground in which feminism could flourish and it was difficult for a women's movement to develop in the context of authoritarian political systems. In Germany, for instance, it was illegal for women to become involved in political meetings or to join political groups. Therefore, the General German Women's Association, founded by Louise Otto in 1865, concentrated on philanthropy and the expansion of educational and employment opportunities. In Russia women's public activity was equated with sexual promiscuity and with oppositional politics and therefore was looked on with suspicion by the state. Nonetheless, women did benefit from the government's modernizing agenda. Educational reforms to ensure that girls would be better mothers had the unintended effect of fostering independence and raising expectations. Feminists were then able to build on this to demand access to higher education. By 1900 women had gained entry to most professions except for the law and, through their work as teachers and doctors, were increasingly seen by the state as a force for stability.

Many countries were still subject to the rule of a foreign power. How far did this affect the growth of a women's movement? To what extent did demands for national autonomy and liberal, representative governments stimulate feminism? Women were often encouraged to take part in nationalist struggles. As mothers, it was assumed that they would educate children in the language and culture of their nation, thereby helping to develop a sense of national identity. It was then only a small step before women began to raise their own demands. Alexandra Gripenberg, a leading feminist in Finland, recognized this connection when she observed that the nationalist movement, by encouraging mothers to teach their children the Finnish language, 'became also an indirect means of awakening the women to a sense of their rights and responsibilities' (Evans 1977: 86). Women involved in nationalist and feminist movements could find their loyalties divided, in particular if they had to make the decision to prioritize one over the other. Nonetheless, in Iceland, Norway and Czechoslovakia women's rights were presented as a nationalist issue and this helped to drive forward the struggle for women's suffrage.

A common sisterhood?

How far did women gain a sense of sisterhood from working together for their rights? Campaigns that challenged their unequal and dependant position highlighted the difficulties that women shared in common. Close friendships, forged in committee work, added an emotional dimension to feminist politics that helped to sustain individuals as they faced hostility and criticism for flouting conventions. A distinct feminist culture developed based on an alternative set of values that included a critique of male conduct and morality. Women did not, however, just move in a female world. They worked closely with male sympathizers, many of whom were family members. In a movement that roused such strong passions and commitment a sense of sisterhood could be fragile. Some women were difficult to work with and others, including the British feminist Elizabeth Wolstenholme Elmy, came under criticism because of their unconventional private lives. Disagreements were frequent and could undermine personal friendships, while class, religion and party political differences could cut across and conflict with a sense of common sisterhood.

Class differences in particular could undermine gender solidarities. In Britain and France feminists argued that they had a common sisterhood with working-class women over the question of employment. They defended women's right to work against attempts by the state, through 'protective legislation', to limit hours of employment or to prohibit women from particular types of work. Drawing parallels with women's exclusion from professional work, they argued that protective legislation was an infringement of women's liberties. Socialist and trade union women took a different view. They looked to legislation and trade unionism as a solution for the long hours and low pay suffered by working women. In the late nineteenth century, when opposition to protective legislation became less pronounced, there was space for greater cooperation between the women's movement and the labour movement.

International sisterhood was also difficult to achieve. News of events and activities in different countries, carried in journals and by propagandists on world-wide speaking tours, did help to stimulate the development of a women's movement, in particular, in places where the political climate was difficult. The establishment of the International Council of Women (ICW) in Washington in 1888, an initiative of the American suffrage leaders Elizabeth Cady Stanton and Susan B. Anthony, then provided the possibility of a more formal link being made. The Council was an umbrella group for a wide range of women's associations and by 1900 ten national councils had affiliated. By aiming to foster unity among its members, however, the ICW avoided controversial issues such as women's suffrage and gained a reputation for moderation and respectability. When the demand for the suffrage became more urgent any pretence at unity collapsed as individuals and groups left the ICW to pursue their interests in other organizations.

Moderates or radicals?

The mainstream women's movement can be characterized as moderate in its aims, ideas and tactics. But this does not tell the whole story. Throughout the period there were dissenting voices, in particular from those who maintained links with an earlier, radical tradition and were prepared to use less conventional methods to achieve their aims. What meanings does the term radical have in the context of the women's movement of the nineteenth century? One of the most influential historians of British suffrage, Sandra Holton, has been instrumental in drawing our attention to a radical tradition within the suffrage movement and has, therefore, changed the way in which it has been viewed. For her, a woman could be defined as a radical if she was impatient with the social conventions of the day, was committed to a radical current of politics outside the women's movement and took up controversial questions such as opposition to the state regulation of prostitution (Holton 1996). In Britain radicals included Elizabeth-Wolstenholme Elmy, the working-class propagandist Jessie Craigen and members of leading Quaker families such as the Brights and the Priestmans. They argued that all women should have the vote, regardless of marital status and attempted to make alliances with working-class women. Some of them refused to pay their rates because they were disenfranchised, while Elizabeth Wolstenholme lived in a 'free union' before being pressurized by members of the women's movement to marry Ben Elmy.

In France and Germany, however, where women's suffrage was viewed as a particularly controversial demand, women could be described as radical largely because they were willing to prioritize the vote. Hubertine Auclert, for instance, criticized the moderate outlook of feminist organizations in France because they did not demand the vote for women. In 1870, therefore, she established her own suffrage group and aimed to attract support from women of all social classes. In common with her British counterparts she carried out direct actions to achieve her aims. With other members of her group she tried to add her name to the electoral roll and, when refused, announced that she would withhold payment of taxes. In the 1880s her broad radicalism went beyond suffrage when she carried out other forms of protest, including attending civil marriage ceremonies where she addressed brides on the iniquities of the marriage law. Auclert founded a magazine, *La Citoyenne*, that lasted from 1881 to 1891, but at this stage she was only able to attract a few hundred women to her organization. The German suffragists Anita Augspurg and Lida Gustava Heymann also established their own suffrage group at the turn of the century. They lived together as a couple and combined suffrage activities with demands for sex reform and work for international peace. Heymann also refused to pay her taxes while she was denied the right to vote.

Feminists not only had different priorities, but also had different understandings about what was meant by women's emancipation and how to achieve it. Early histories of feminism tried to make sense of these differences by identifying strands – in a pioneering study Olive Banks, for example, pointed to an equal rights, an evangelical and a socialist tradition in British feminism (Banks 1980). Feminists certainly had different ideas and strategies, but attempting to fit them too neatly into strands can be constraining. Individuals could draw on a complex set of ideas that often cut across each other and changed as alliances, priorities and tactics shifted over time.

John Stuart Mill and August Bebel

Two key texts that helped to stimulate debates on the 'woman question' and provided a framework of ideas for feminists to

---

BOX 2.6

John Stuart Mill (1806–73)

Born in London, the eldest son of the philosopher and economist James Mill, John Stuart Mill became an eminent liberal philosopher and politician. He was influenced in his intellectual development by Harriet Taylor, a married woman with whom he began a long friendship in 1830. They married in 1851 after the death of her husband and in the same year she published an article on 'The Enfranchisement of Women' in the *Westminster Review*. They moved in radical intellectual circles that were sympathetic to re-thinking the social position of women, but it was not until after his wife's death that Mill began to write his book, *On the Subjection of Women*, published in 1869. It was to be a groundbreaking work proposing the legal and political emancipation of women.

On a practical level, Mill, who was elected as an MP in 1865, furthered the cause of women's suffrage by proposing an amendment to the Second Reform Bill in 1867, although this was defeated. With his stepdaughter, Helen Taylor, he played an important, and sometimes controversial role in the London women's suffrage movement and in 1872 became the nominal president of the London National Society for Women's Suffrage.

---

use, were both written by men. One was John Stuart Mill's *The Subjection of Women* (1869).

Mill rejected the view that women were biologically inferior to men and argued that their social upbringing was responsible for any special characteristics that they displayed. Only if women were able to develop fully as human beings, free of legal and cultural restrictions, would it be possible to know what women's nature was really like. Mill emphasized the importance of individual 'self development and the cultivation of individual faculties' and insisted that women should be able to play a full part in political life (Rendall 2001: 172). Mill's ideas were not always in tune with those of the women's movement. He criticized marriage as a form of slavery for women, but did not challenge the sex division of labour and assumed that women with young children would remain within the home. He also said little about single women, who were central to the concerns of the nineteenth-century women's movement. Mill assumed that domesticity made women unsuited for public roles and, therefore, they needed to be exposed to public life before they could participate in it. This was in complete contrast to feminists who argued that the skills and qualities developed by women within the home qualified them for public and political life.

Contemporaries therefore had mixed reactions to his book but it had a considerable impact that went beyond Britain. In the first year of publication it appeared in the United States, Australia and New Zealand and in translation in France, Germany, Austria, Sweden and Denmark. The leading Italian women's rights advocate, Maria Mozzoni, translated Mill's book, while in 1884 the Finnish Women's Association was founded by a group of women in Helsinki who had met to discuss Mill's ideas. The Association demanded equal rights in education and employment, sought legislation to end the double standard of morality and supported the demand for votes for women.

A second key text, based on a very different set of political assumptions and ideas, was *Woman and Socialism* (1879) written by August Bebel, a leader of the influential German Social Democratic Party (SPD). Bebel argued that a woman in capitalist society was doubly disadvantaged since she suffered economic and social dependence on a man within the family as well as from economic exploitation at the workplace. He explored the social construction of gender and claimed that the 'domination of women by men was rooted not in biology but in history and was thus capable of resolution in history' (Sowerwine 1987: 403). On the other hand, by using economic definitions of class to describe women's role within the family, or a sex/class analogy, he argued that women would only gain emancipation if they worked alongside men to achieve a socialist society. Bebel's writings provided 'no clear space to develop an understanding of patriarchy, as either a separate or a related system to capitalism' (Hunt 1996: 25) and, therefore, had an ambivalent and contradictory impact on the socialist construction of the woman question. By asserting the primacy of class he enabled socialists to marginalize women's concerns, but by recognizing that women had specific experiences he also ensured that the woman question would be debated extensively in socialist circles.

Bebel's book was translated into several languages and went into numerous editions. His ideas about the relationship between sex and class were then developed further by Clara Zetkin, a leader of the women's section of the German SPD.

She popularized her views in a pamphlet on the woman question in 1889 and through her editorship of the newspaper *Die Gleichheit* (Equality), first published in 1891. In 1896 she made an influential speech at the Congress of the Socialist Second International[1] where, while sympathetic to the aims of the 'bourgeois women's movement', she opposed any attempts to cooperate with them and set out to show that the interests of women workers lay with their class. In practice, however, socialist women adopted a variety of strategies to achieve their goals; they challenged the preoccupation of their own organizations with the interests of the male worker and sought to foreground the specific needs of women. They also, on occasion, joined with 'bourgeois' women over specific campaigns.

Irrespective of any differences in political perspective, feminists did share a number of common assumptions. They recognized that it was crucial to contest contemporary definitions of masculinity and femininity and to engage in what Offen describes as 'knowledge wars' (Offen 2000). They denied that women were suited only for domestic life and challenged the liberal assumption that the private world of the home was separate from the public world of work. In doing so they drew upon the language of liberalism and socialism to condemn the restrictions that women faced, but added a new dimension by addressing the 'central question of sexual oppression, as distinct from political or social oppression' (Caine 1992: 41). They also demonstrated how work and family roles structured female subordination. In demanding a role for women outside the home feminists used Victorian domestic ideology and notions of sexual difference to their own advantage. If women possessed distinct virtues and values then these needed to be used for the good of society as a whole and justified a role for women in public life. Negotiating this complex relationship between 'equality' and 'difference' was something feminists continued to do well beyond the nineteenth century.

At the start of the new century the women's movement in Europe and North America was many faceted. Despite disagreements over theory, tactics and strategies feminists did share many similarities as they confronted a common set of ideas about women's nature and their social roles. As well as seeking equal rights for women in employment, education and the law, they also claimed a role for women in public life on the basis of sexual difference and the positive qualities possessed by their sex. They challenged male dominance, or patriarchy, in all spheres of life, exposed male violence within the family and contested the double standard of morality. By 1900 women in most countries had greater access to education and professional employment, while married women had an improved legal status. These changes were achieved through a combination of feminist campaigns and broader economic and social developments, including the willingness of some governments to improve women's education in the interests of the state. The one demand that still remained elusive, however, was the right to vote, and at the end of the nineteenth century this increasingly came to the foreground of feminist campaigning.

Further reading

For a discussion of the complex origins of modern feminism, see Jane Rendall, *The Origins of Modern Feminism: Women in Britain, France and the United States, 1780–1860*, Basingstoke:

Macmillan, 1985; and Karen Offen, *European Feminisms, 1780–1950: A Political History*, Stanford, CA: Stanford University Press, 2000.

The ideas of the Enlightenment are explained in Dorinda Outram, *The Enlightenment*, Cambridge: Cambridge University Press, 1995.

The impact of the French Revolution is explored in Rendall and Offen, above. See also James F. McMillan, *France and Women, 1789–1914. Gender, Society and Politics*, London: Routledge, 2000; Barbara Caine and Glenda Sluga, *Gendering European History*, London: Leicester University Press, 2000; and Gisela Bock, *Women in European History*, Oxford: Blackwell, 2002.

Mary Wollstonecraft's ideas have been the subject of extensive debate and differing interpretations. For a recent discussion of her work, see Eileen Janes Yeo (ed.) *Mary Wollstonecraft and 200 Years of Feminisms*, London: Rivers Oram, 1997; and Barbara Taylor, *Mary Wollstonecraft and the Feminist Imagination*, Cambridge: Cambridge University Press, 2003.

Lee Holcombe, *Wives and Property: Reform of the Married Women's Property Law in Nineteenth Century England*, Toronto: University of Toronto Press, 1983, provides a detailed account of women's legal position. For an overview of the social and economic changes affecting women during industrialization and a guide to further reading, see Katrina Honeyman, *Women, Gender and Industrialisation in England, 1700–1870*, Basingstoke: Macmillan, 2000. An influential text exploring family, separate spheres and class is: Leonore Davidoff and Catherine Hall, *Family Fortunes. Men and Women of the English Middle Class, 1750–1850*, London: Hutchinson, 1987. For a recent critique of their ideas, see Amanda Vickery, 'Golden Age to Separate Spheres? A Review of the Categories and Chronology of English Women's History', *Historical Journal*, 36, 1993.

The argument that women in the late eighteenth and nineteenth centuries remained active in the public sphere and that the women's movement was an attempt to extend this role is explored in: Kathryn Gleadle and Sarah Richardson (eds) *Women in British Politics, 1760–1860. The Power of the Petticoat*, Basingstoke: Macmillan, 2000; and in Kathryn Gleadle, 'British Women and radical Politics in the Late Nonconformist Enlightenment, c. 1780–1830', in Amanda Vickery (ed.) *Women, Privilege and Power. British Politics, 1750 to the Present*, Stanford, CA: Stanford University Press, 2001. They also raise questions about what should be defined as political. Ann Summers gives greater emphasis to the restrictions that women faced. See *Female Lives, Moral States*, Newbury: Threshold Press, 2000.

For an overview of women's involvement in philanthropy, temperance and anti-slavery campaigns in the United States and a guide to further reading, see Jay Kleinberg, *Women in American Society, 1820–1920*, Brighton: British Association for American Studies, Pamphlet 20, 1990; and Christine Bolt, *The Women's Movements in the United States and Britain from the 1790s to the 1920s*, Hemel Hempstead: Harvester Wheatsheaf, 1993. The relationship between anti-slavery campaigns, colonialism and the development of the women's movement in Britain is explored in: Clare Midgley, *Women Against Slavery: The British Campaigns, 1780–1870*, London, Routledge, 1992; and Clare Midgley, 'British Women, Women's Rights and Empire, 1790–1850', in Patricia Grimshaw, K. Holmes and Marilyn Lake (eds) *Women's Rights and Human Rights*, Basingstoke: Palgrave, 2001. For a local example, see June Hannam, ' "An Enlarged Sphere

of Usefulness": The Bristol Women's Movement, c. 1860–1914',
in Madge Dresser and Philip Ollerenshaw (eds) *The Making of
Modern Bristol*, Tiverton: Redcliffe Press, 1996.

The most stimulating discussion of the relationship between
utopian socialism and women's emancipation is still Barbara
Taylor, *Eve and the New Jerusalem. Socialism and Feminism in the
Nineteenth Century*, London: Virago, 1983. For France, see Susan
Grogan, *Flora Tristan: Life Stories*, London: Routledge, 1998.

The campaigns against state regulation and social purity are
discussed in: Judith Walkowitz, *Prostitution and Victorian Society:
Women, Class and the State*, Cambridge: Cambridge University
Press, 1980; Ute Frevert, *Women in German History: From Bourgeois
Emancipation to Sexual Liberation*, Oxford: Berg, 1989; Lucy Bland,
*Banishing the Beast: English Feminism and Sexual Morality, 1885–
1914*, Harmondsworth: Penguin, 1995.

The relationship between liberal nationalism and women's
rights in Europe is explored in Richard J. Evans, *The Feminists:
Women's Emancipation Movements in Europe, America and Australasia,
1840–1920*, London: Croom Helm, 1977. For the women's move-
ment in individual countries, see Linda Edmondson, 'Women's
Rights, Gender and Citizenship in Tsarist Russia, 1860–1920: The
Question of Difference', in Grimshaw, Holmes and Lake (eds)
Women's Rights and Human Rights; Ute Gerhard, 'The Women's
Movement in Germany', in Gabriele Griffin and Rosi Braidotti
(eds) *Thinking Differently: A Reader in European Women's Studies*,
London: Zed Books, 2002; Steven C. Hause with Anne R. Kenney,
Women's Suffrage and Social Politics in the French Third Republic,
Princeton, NJ: Princeton University Press, 1984; and Eleanor
Flexner, *Century of Struggle: The Woman's Rights Movement in the
United States*, Cambridge, MA: Harvard University Press, 1959.

Women's friendships are discussed in Philippa Levine, 'Love, Friendship and Feminism in Later Nineteenth-Century England', *Women's Studies International Forum*, 13, 1/2, 1990. For the international links, see Leila J. Rupp, *Worlds of Women: The Making of an International Women's Movement*, Princeton, NJ: Princeton University Press, 1997. Sandra Stanley Holton, *Suffrage Days: Stories from the Women's Suffrage Movement*, London: Routledge, 1996, argues that there was a continuity between nineteenth-century radicalism in Britain and the militancy of the Edwardian suffrage movement.

Olive Banks, *Faces of Feminism*, Oxford: Martin Robertson, 1980 was one of the first historians to identify separate strands in the women's movement. This view was later challenged by historians who argued that feminist ideas were complex and that there were interconnections between individuals and movements. For example, see Barbara Caine, *Victorian Feminism*, Oxford: Oxford University Press, 1992. For a discussion of John Stuart Mill's ideas, see Jane Rendall, *Origins*; and 'John Stuart Mill, Liberal Politics, and the Movements for Women's Suffrage, 1865–1873', in Vickery (ed.) *Women, Privilege and Power*. For the impact of socialist ideas on nineteenth-century debates around the 'woman question', see Karen Honeycut, 'Clara Zetkin: A Socialist Approach to the Problem of Women's Oppression', in Jane Slaughter and Robert Kern (eds) *European Women on the Left*, Westport, CT: Greenwood Press, 1981; June Hannam and Karen Hunt, *Socialist Women. Britain 1880s to 1920s*, London: Routledge, 2001; Ellen C. DuBois, 'Woman Suffrage and the Left: An International Socialist-Feminist Perspective', *New Left Review*, 186, 1991; Charles Sowerwine, 'The Socialist Women's Movement from 1850–1940', in Renate Bridenthal,

Claudia Koontz and Susan Stuard (eds) *Becoming Visible: Women in European History*, Boston: Houghton Mifflin, 1987; and Karen Hunt, *Equivocal Feminists. The Social Democratic Federation and the Woman Question, 1884–1911*, Cambridge: Cambridge University Press, 1996.

Note

1 The Second International (1889–1914) was an umbrella group to which European socialist parties affiliated. Its congresses provided the opportunity for representatives to meet and formulate policy that would guide, rather than bind, its members.

CHAPTER 3

Women's suffrage, 1860s–1920s

WHY WAS WOMEN'S SUFFRAGE such a controversial issue and why did it take so long to achieve? Why did women want the vote so badly and why has it had such a central place in histories of feminism? To what extent did suffrage campaigns make a difference to the achievement of the vote? Both supporters and opponents believed that women would use the vote to bring about social and political change. But more than that contemporaries feared that if women had a political voice then the 'traditional' relationship between men and women in the family and the workplace would come under threat. Feminists certainly recognized the symbolic importance of the vote. It signified the possibility of women acting together across national boundaries to transform the world in which they lived. This helps to explain why it evoked such strong feelings on both sides.

Sex was a key factor in deciding who should, or should not, be included in the franchise. The demand for women's suffrage, therefore, highlighted women's common interests and raised the possibility of a 'universal sisterhood'. It was the one issue that brought women from a variety of backgrounds together in organized groups and in highly public campaigns. This in turn could foster a sense of solidarity among women as they faced intransigent opposition to their cause. Organized suffrage movements developed first in the 'liberal democracies' of Europe, North America and the white-settler colonies of Australia and New Zealand and in most cases reached a peak in the decade before the First World War. Given their size and 'militancy', the British and American movements took centre stage among contemporaries and also in later suffrage histories. But this should not lead us to neglect suffrage movements in other countries. They had their own priorities, aims and tactics which need to be recognized and should not simply be viewed through the eyes of Anglo-American campaigners.

Origins of women's suffrage campaigns

The first women's suffrage organizations were formed in the 1860s in the context of broader political developments. Although women's suffrage was raised in the United States at the Seneca Falls Convention in 1848, it was not until the Civil War that organizations were formed at state level with the specific aim of campaigning for the vote. Once hostilities were over, two national groups were established: the National Woman Suffrage Association, led by Elizabeth Cady Stanton and Susan B. Anthony, and the American Woman Suffrage Association led by Lucy Stone. In Britain women raised their own demands when working-class men, who were excluded from a property-based franchise, campaigned for political reforms in the late 1860s.

BOX 3.1

Susan B. Anthony (1820–1906) and Elizabeth Cady Stanton (1815–1902)

Susan B. Anthony and Elizabeth Cady Stanton were leading figures in the nineteenth-century women's suffrage movement in America and their example inspired women throughout the world. Both women were influenced by the movement to abolish slavery. The daughter of a cotton mill owner, Anthony was born into a Quaker household that supported abolition and temperance. Elizabeth Cady was the daughter of a judge and married the abolitionist leader Henry Stanton. She attended the World Anti-Slavery Convention in London where women were excluded on the grounds of their sex and this influenced her later decision, along with Lucretia Mott, to call the first women's rights convention at Seneca Falls in 1848.

Anthony and Stanton met in 1851. This was the start of a lifelong association and close friendship. They established a journal, *The Revolution*, in 1868 and in the following year formed the National Woman Suffrage Association. This marked a rift with the abolitionist movement since Anthony and Stanton opposed the Fifteenth Amendment which enfranchised black men but excluded women. They also took the initiative in founding the International Council of Women in 1888 to foster international solidarity. In 1890 Stanton was elected as the first president of the National American Woman Suffrage Association, but by this time her influence as a political activist was waning and she retired in 1892. Anthony took over as president, a post she held until 1900. Stanton is also remembered for her writings. With Joslyn Gage she published a three-volume *History of Woman Suffrage* (1886) and in 1896 produced the controversial text, *The Woman's Bible*.

Women's suffrage societies were formed in large provincial cities as well as in London and in 1868 these joined together in a loose federation called the National Society for Women's Suffrage.

In Australia, New Zealand, France, Canada and Scandinavia an organized movement for women's suffrage developed slightly later, in the 1880s and 90s, and the numbers involved tended to be small. In New Zealand the Woman's Christian Temperance Union (WCTU) took up the suffrage question. One of its leaders, Kate Sheppard, promoted press campaigns and produced suffrage literature, while the WCTU put strong pressure on parliament by sending in resolutions and petitions. Similarly in Australia the WCTU began to canvass support for women's suffrage in 1888 and was then joined by the Womanhood Suffrage League, formed by Rose Scott in 1891.

In Scandinavia and parts of the Austro-Hungarian Empire there were close connections between liberal nationalist movements and women's suffrage. In Norway, for example, Gina Krog, who was inspired by events in the United States, formed the Female Suffrage Union in 1885. But it was not until radical liberal nationalists, who thought that women would support them in their goal of independence from Sweden, took up the demand for women's suffrage in the 1890s that it became a key political issue. Women who took part in nationalist struggles and were inspired to demand political rights for themselves often found that their own needs were neglected once national independence had been achieved. But this was not invariably the case. In Finland and Norway women gained the vote in 1906 and 1913 respectively and this was closely related to their support for the nationalist movement. Similarly in Czechoslovakia women who took part in the nationalist movement in the 1890s began to raise demands on behalf of their sex. They organized a petition for women's suffrage and in 1905 Františka Plamínková formed the Committee for Women's Suffrage. Women used the argument that their demands were integral to Czech democratic traditions, which were contrasted with those of more repressive governments. They benefited from the support of the liberal nationalist leader Masaryk, president of the post-war republic that introduced women's suffrage.

It was difficult for women to demand the vote in countries with authoritarian political systems. Nonetheless, the departure of the German Chancellor, Bismarck, in 1890 did create a space for groups demanding liberal reforms. The Federation of German Women's Associations, formed in 1894, did not at first include women's suffrage in its official programme. The affiliated groups had such a wide range of aims that the Federation only represented views acceptable to the majority. Once Marie Stritt became president in 1899, however, women's suffrage was pushed higher up the agenda. In Russia women were inspired to demand the suffrage as part of the political upheavals of the period 1904–5, when the Tsar was forced to call a Duma (parliament) and also by the success of the women's suffrage movement in Finland. Women were so infuriated by their exclusion from the Duma that they formed the All-Russian Union of Equal Rights for Women, led by professional and literary women in Moscow, to achieve equality before the law, including voting rights.

Many moderate women's associations, especially in countries outside Britain and North America, concentrated on civil rather than political rights. They were reluctant to include women's suffrage in their aims because it was seen as a particularly radical demand. Those women who became frustrated with this cautious outlook and wanted to prioritize the vote had to form their own organizations. In France, for example, Hubertine Auclert broke her association with the moderate feminists and formed Suffrage des femmes (Women's Suffrage) in 1876. Similarly in Denmark a minority of members of the Danish Women's Association left to form suffrage groups in the mid-1880s, while Gina Krog left the Norwegian Feminist Society, whose members showed little interest in participating in politics, to form the Female Suffrage Union in 1885.

As noted in Chapter 2, however, the term radical could have multiple meanings. Just to take up the cause of women's suffrage could be seen as radical in some countries. In others, where the campaign for the vote was stronger, there were differences between suffrage supporters themselves. Gina Krog, for example, can be seen as a moderate because she advocated a property-based franchise, even after adult suffrage for men had been achieved, since she believed that the middle-class parties of the Norwegian parliament would be more likely to enfranchise women of their own class. In Britain the term radical has been used to describe different groups of suffrage supporters. Sandra Holton, for example, has traced a radical strand of suffragism throughout the nineteenth century (see Chapter 2) whereas Jill Liddington and Jill Norris (1978), in a pioneering and influential study, use the term radical suffragist in a very specific way to describe Lancashire working-class women at the turn of the century. Rejecting the demand for votes for women on the same terms as men, which would have enfranchised propertied women, in favour of a demand for womanhood suffrage to include all women, they saw women's suffrage as inextricably linked to the broader aims of the labour movement and sought to build a mass movement of working women. What this shows is the importance of exercising caution in the use of terms such as radical or moderate and being clear about their meaning in specific contexts.

Why did women face so much opposition to their claim for the vote? Opponents identified women with the domestic world and argued that they were simply unsuited to make decisions about imperial affairs or foreign policy. It was feared that their 'womanliness' would be jeopardized and that male authority within the family would be threatened. Ridicule was used to undermine suffrage supporters. Cartoonists, such as Jules Grandjouan in France, used their drawings to show that the vote would bring domestic chaos and to depict suffragists as unsexed, mannish creatures. Women who opposed the suffrage used similar arguments and formed their own organizations against female enfranchisement.

Ideas of suffragists and the meaning of citizenship

Suffragists had to respond to these criticisms when making their own case for the vote. They argued that women should have the vote as a natural right based on their common humanity with men and believed that they could not be fully human unless they had citizenship rights. For some the claim to political rights was rooted in property ownership, whereas for others it rested on humanity alone, that is the individual's ability to reason. By demanding that women should have a role as active citizens in formal political life, suffragists challenged the ideology of separate spheres at the heart of liberal political thought. At the same time they drew on gender differences to support their case by arguing that women would bring particular qualities to politics, and demanded that 'their differences from men should be acknowledged in their citizenship' (Pateman 1992: 19). In doing so they denied that enfranchisement would undermine 'womanliness'. Instead they argued that their 'womanliness' could be used in the service of the community.

On the surface it might seem that there was a dichotomy between arguments based on equal rights and those based on women's difference from men, but the ideas put forward were complex and interlinking rather than mutually exclusive. Liberalism itself emphasized civic responsibilities, combining the notion of individual rights with the language of duty, responsibility and public service. Women simply re-worked this to suit their own purposes. Millicent Fawcett, a leader of the British suffrage movement, was typical of many in arguing that the right to vote would not only contribute to women's self-development and personal fulfilment, but would also lead to an unselfish public spirit in which women could help those less fortunate than themselves.

Equal rights was always central to the arguments used by suffragists to demand the vote, but after the turn of the century there was a change in emphasis. Politicians and social commentators increasingly saw motherhood as vital for the strength of the nation and the future of the 'race'. Suffragists then took up these issues when making their own demands. They argued that women, with their maternal and domestic qualities, would support reforms to help women and children and would seek to achieve a moral regeneration of society. Up to a point anti-suffrage women shared similar attitudes about women's active

BOX 3.2

Millicent Garrett Fawcett (1847–1929)

As president of the National Union of Women's Suffrage Societies, Millicent Fawcett was the leader of the constitutionalist wing of the British suffrage movement from the late 1890s. Born in Suffolk, the daughter of a successful Liberal middle-class businessman, she married the blind MP, Henry Fawcett. Through her sister Elizabeth, who was to qualify as the first woman doctor in England, she was brought in touch with feminist circles in London in the 1870s and took part in campaigning for married women's legal rights as well as writing and speaking on the subject of women's suffrage. After the death of her husband in 1884 she concentrated on working tirelessly for women's suffrage. Under her leadership the NUWSS grew in strength in the period before the First World War. There was controversy within the NUWSS over her decision to form an alliance with the Labour Party in 1912, thereby breaking the non-party-political position of the organization, and over her support for the war effort. The NUWSS remained intact, however, and towards the end of the war played an important role in ensuring that women would be included in proposals to extend the franchise. Fawcett was a pragmatic campaigner who worked within the political system to achieve her aims. She resigned the presidency of the NUWSS in 1919 and was made a Dame Grand Cross order of the British Empire in 1925. She lived long enough to witness all women gaining the franchise in 1928.

citizenship. They feared that women voters would have little say in a male dominated political world but they were anxious to ensure that women could exert influence in other ways. The Women's Anti-Suffrage League, formed in London in 1908, argued strongly that women, as mothers, should play a key role in Britain's 'imperial destiny' since the 'whole "future of the race" turned upon women's caring work in their home and communities' (Bush 2002: 433). Their involvement in social welfare work and 'enthusiasm for advancing women's interests' meant that anti suffragists could work alongside moderate suffragists, despite their differences on the franchise question.

Both groups of women were ethnocentric in their outlook and in the meaning that they gave to women's citizenship. In Britain, for example, suffragists and anti suffragists argued that women had a role to play in the Empire through their civilizing mission that would mitigate the harsher aspects of colonial rule and therefore strengthen the Empire. Suffragists saw themselves, in liberal terms, as part of a 'progressive movement of civilization' that could be measured by the improvements that had occurred in women's social position. They believed that they could take the lead in encouraging women's emancipation in the colonies and also that their own enfranchisement would enable them to press for reforms to improve the lives of indigenous populations of the Empire. Suffragists talked of reaching out to their suffering sisters, but there were limits to the extent to which they could connect with women in the colonies on equal terms. Indeed, they were most likely to view themselves as part of a mother–daughter relationship, with the unequal positions of power that this entailed, and to construct a picture of Indian women as helpless victims of oppression rather than as active participants in political struggles to improve their social position.

Women in Western societies were, therefore, often complicit with the racism of colonial regimes at home and abroad. Australian feminists, for instance, were so keen to join the nation that they colluded with racism when they accepted the exclusion

women, in particular, in New York, where trade union leaders such as Rose Schneiderman and Leonora O'Reilly spoke on suffrage platforms.

Similarly in Britain provincial organizations came together in 1897 to form the National Union of Women's Suffrage Societies (NUWSS) under the leadership of Millicent Fawcett. The basis of support began to widen. Women who had taken advantage of greater educational opportunities and were employed in the expanding areas of teaching, nursing and clerical work took up the suffrage cause alongside some groups of industrial workers. In Lancashire, where textile workers took the lead, new methods of campaigning were used, including open-air meetings, leafleting at factory gates and public demonstrations, while in 1900 29,300 signatures were obtained for a suffrage petition.

Elsewhere in Europe, including Germany, France, Denmark and Sweden, new organizations were formed. Membership was smaller that in Britain and the United States but should not be underestimated. The German Union for Women's Suffrage, established by Anita Augspurg and Lida Heymann in 1902, had only 2,500 members by 1908, but when the ban on women's participation in politics was lifted in that year its membership expanded rapidly and reached 9,000 by 1913. In Denmark the two largest suffrage groups had 23,000 members between them by 1910, a significant proportion of the small female population of 1.5 million. Here a broad coalition of women's organizations supported the campaign for the vote, including nurses, teachers, girl scouts and deaconesses associations as well as the suffrage groups themselves. They also managed to cooperate with women from trade unions and the Social Democratic Party.

The fresh lease of life gained by the women's suffrage movement could also be seen at an international level. For the first
time a transnational organization devoted to the campaign for
the vote was established. The International Woman Suffrage
Alliance (IWSA) was formed in Berlin in 1904 after the International Council of Women (ICW) failed to give wholehearted
support to the suffrage cause. The aim of the IWSA was to act as
a central bureau to collect, exchange and disseminate information about suffrage work and to stimulate national suffrage
activities. Congresses were held every two years until the outbreak of war and members were kept in touch through the
IWSA journal, *Jus Suffragii*. National women's suffrage organizations that had suffrage as a sole objective could affiliate to the
IWSA. The definition of a national group was ambiguous, however, and led to controversy in later years when there were splits
in national suffrage movements. It was agreed that suffrage
would be pursued as a matter of human rights and justice.
This contrasted with the emphasis of some national groups on
women's special qualities, derived from the domestic sphere,
as a justification for the vote.

Men also gave their support. Politicians raised the issue
in parliament and journalists used their access to the media
to spread suffrage propaganda. Tom Johnston, editor of the
Scottish socialist newspaper *Forward*, and the Czech nationalist
leader Tomas Masaryk, editor of *Our Era*, both gave sympathetic
coverage to women's suffrage in their newspapers, while others,
such as Henry Blackwell and Frederick Pethick-Lawrence,
edited suffrage papers jointly with their wives. Married couples
had often worked together for political or social reform, but
the suffrage movement did provide a different context for this

shared activity and challenged the roles that men and women were expected to play.

The struggle for the vote was a female-dominated movement with leadership firmly in the hands of women. Male supporters were expected to be in an auxiliary position. In France, for example, the suffrage movement was largely comprised of women by 1900, with men forming approximately 15–20% of the membership of feminist societies compared to almost half earlier in the century (Hause with Kenney 1984: 44). Some suffrage groups excluded men from holding office while others were closed to men altogether, including the British Women's Social and Political Union, the Norwegian Female Suffrage Union, the NWSA in America and the Female Progressive Association in Denmark. In a number of countries, therefore, men established their own organizations to support the campaign for women's suffrage and in 1912 groups from The Netherlands, France, Sweden, Britain, Hungary, the United States and Denmark came together to form the Men's International Alliance for Woman Suffrage.

Militancy

In the decade before the First World War the British suffrage movement took centre stage as 'militant' methods caught women's imagination throughout the world. Militancy has given us the most enduring images of the campaign – women being arrested and forcibly fed – that are instantly recognizable to a wide public. Britain, rather than the United States, was now looked to for leadership and inspiration from women in other countries who faced greater political and social restrictions on

BOX 3.4

Emmeline Pankhurst (1858–1928)

Emmeline Pankhurst was the most well known, charismatic leader of the British militant movement. The daughter of a manufacturer, Robert Goulden, she married the radical lawyer Richard Pankhurst in 1879. They were involved in a range of radical causes, including women's rights campaigns and in the 1890s joined the socialist group, the Independent Labour Party. Emmeline withdrew from politics after Richard's sudden death in 1898 in order to earn a living to support her children, but in 1903 formed the Women's Social and Political Union. As the women's suffrage movement began to gain momentum, she threw herself wholeheartedly into the struggle, carrying out propaganda throughout the country. Emmeline suffered a great deal for her beliefs. Between 1908 and the outbreak of war she took part in demonstrations and deputations that led to her repeated arrest and imprisonment, and she had to endure forcible feeding on numerous occasions. Her physical courage inspired devotion from her followers and gave her the status of a 'heroine'. Her single-mindedness could also cause rifts with close friends and colleagues, including Emmeline and Frederick Pethick-Lawrence. All of her children supported women's rights, although her son Harry died tragically young in 1910. Her daughters, Christabel (1880–1958), Adela (1885–1961) and Sylvia (1882–1960) were all active in the WSPU but Adela and Sylvia's continuing commitment to socialism caused a rift with their mother.

When war was declared, Emmeline gave wholehearted support to the government and in the 1920s joined the Conservative Party. After her death, a bronze statue was erected in Victoria Tower gardens in memory of her contribution to the suffrage cause.

their activities and their lives. The new tactics were initiated by the Women's Social and Political Union (WSPU), an organization established in 1903 by Emmeline Pankhurst, along with other members of the Manchester branch of the socialist group, the Independent Labour Party.

Inspired by the suffrage activities of women workers in Lancashire they sought initially to carry out propaganda for socialism and for suffrage and for two years remained as a small, locally based group. All this was to change in 1905 when the WSPU came into the limelight in a dramatic way. During the General Election campaign of that year two WSPU members, Annie Kenney and Christabel Pankhurst, disrupted a meeting by shouting Votes for Women and were promptly arrested. This led to further disruptive activities, including heckling speakers and mass lobbying of parliament, as well as to the organization of large demonstrations and processions in London. Other organizations followed suit, including the Women's Freedom League (WFL), a breakaway group formed in 1907 by Teresa Billington-Greig and Charlotte Despard. As frustration mounted the WSPU, whose members were called suffragettes to distinguish them from those who used constitutional methods (see Box 3.5), escalated their tactics. Their new campaign involved the smashing of windows, setting fire to empty buildings and destroying mail in post boxes. Approximately 1,000 women were imprisoned for their suffrage activities and after 1909 many went on hunger strike to protest at being denied the status of political prisoners. They were forcibly fed and in 1913 the 'Cat and Mouse' Act enabled the government to release prisoners until their health had recovered and then to re-arrest them.

BOX 3.5

Suffragette and suffragist – a definition

Suffragette

Suffragette was first used as a pejorative term by the *Daily Mail* on 10 January 1906 to describe members of the WSPU who were disrupting the election meetings of Winston Churchill, a prospective Liberal minister. The WSPU then adopted the word to describe themselves, although it was soon used more widely to include all those who engaged in militant activities. The WSPU published a newspaper entitled *Suffragette* between 1912 and 1915.

Suffragist

Suffragist was used from the nineteenth century to refer to women and men who supported the movement for women's suffrage. In the immediate pre-war years it was applied more specifically to those who used constitutional or legal methods in contrast to the militants.

The terms suffragette and suffragist were used both by contemporaries and subsequently by historians.

Militancy has always provoked passionate debate. Suffrage campaigners, for example, disagreed about whether militancy was effective or legitimate. In their autobiographies, often written in the inter-war years, suffragettes associated militancy with destruction of property, imprisonment and hunger striking which has had a long lasting influence on the way the public and historians have looked at the movement (Kean 1994; Mayhall 2003). But, how should we define militancy? What did it mean to those who took part? If we look closely at the different organizations and individual activists then it becomes clear that militant actions were very diverse and also changed over time. When WSPU members first heckled cabinet ministers at meetings their action was considered as militant, but this was a far cry from the window breaking and arson that was a feature of the campaign just before the war. WFL members looked for other ways to express their militancy that did not involve the destruction of property, including tax resistance and a boycott of the 1911 census. Within the WSPU itself women could choose which type of activity they wanted to engage in and not all volunteered for 'active service'. It was less a question of whether a specific activity was undertaken and more a matter of the spirit in which women approached their political activism. The intensity of feeling and the daring of suffragettes inspired women from a variety of social and political backgrounds to give up everything for the cause and transformed the lives of those who took part. For suffragettes, militancy was a way of expressing active citizenship, perhaps best encapsulated in the phrase, 'Deeds not Words', the motto of the WSPU. In the early years, in particular, many women were members of both the WSPU and the NUWSS, while other organizations such as the Actresses' Franchise League and the Writers' and Artists' Franchise League cooperated with both groups.

The terms constitutionalist and militant provide us with useful labels to distinguish between different tactics and strategies, but they do not describe completely distinct positions. In the early years many women belonged to several different groups at once and they influenced each other. Inspired by the flamboyance of the WSPU, the NUWSS changed its methods and held large demonstrations, pageants and processions, including the

1913 Pilgrimage in which thousands of women marched from all over Britain to a rally in London. The NUWSS found new ways to spread ideas, such as the suffrage caravan in which speakers toured through towns and villages. Suffrage activists may have disagreed about the effectiveness of militancy, but the publicity generated by the campaign boosted the membership of all suffrage groups.[1]

In France Madeleine Pelletier and Caroline Kauffman disrupted meetings by showering delegates with leaflets, while in China members of the Women's Suffrage Alliance armed themselves with pistols and stormed the parliament for three days. The Irish Women's Franchise League harassed visiting English politicians, resisted the 1911 census and in 1912 began to smash windows, leading to the arrest and imprisonment of those who took part. The American, Alice Paul, who had been arrested while living in London, introduced militant methods when she returned to the United States, including a picket of the White House. The WSPU clearly inspired these actions, but in most countries outside Britain they were confined to a minority.

Using propaganda such as posters, plays, novels and newspapers suffragettes countered the view that engagement in politics would make women less womanly. In place of the embittered, masculine spinster or the domineering wife that appeared in the imagery of their opponents, they put the womanly woman who protected the interests of working-class women and children or the educated professional woman such as the teacher, nurse or midwife. They also used Joan of Arc and other well-known historical figures to represent powerful women operating in a political context. Propaganda, in particular imagery, was a powerful tool to challenge contemporary notions of how women should behave and of what it meant to be a 'political' woman. It became an important part of the suffrage campaign in other countries of the world, although the imagery was not always the same. In Austria and Germany it reflected a more 'traditional' view of femininity since suffragists were anxious to counter arguments that women would become too masculine if they entered politics. In contrast, socialist women highlighted women's strength and bravery. They were prepared to take to the streets to gain the suffrage. A poster advertising Women's Day in Germany's red week, March 1914, depicted a woman of strength, who was bare-footed and plainly dressed, holding a flag and standing above the slogan 'Come Out For Women's Right to Vote'. Thus suffrage campaigners both used, and subverted, contemporary definitions of femininity and adopted those images which best suited their particular national contexts.

The campaign for the vote also generated intense debate about the causes of women's subordination, the meaning of emancipation and what feminists hoped to do once they were enfranchised. A minority of radical feminists criticized the constraints of marriage and, inspired by sexual psychologists such as Havelock Ellis, took an interest in sexual freedom and pleasure for women. The mainstream suffrage movement was also interested in sexual issues and saw them as linked to the vote. But they remained suspicious of demands for greater sexual freedom and called instead for men to exercise self control and for an end to the double standard of morality. Fearing the spread of venereal disease, the WSPU came up with the well known slogan 'Votes for women, chastity for men'. Christabel Pankhurst and other members of the Union saw male power over women as encompassing personal as well as political and economic life and argued that women's exclusion from politics left them powerless in their sexual lives. Controversially, they drew a parallel between married women's exchange of sexual services for economic support with the prostitute's sale of her body and sex to male clients.

Socialism and suffrage

If some feminists increasingly emphasized male power over women, others continued to focus on class as well as sex oppression and drew attention to the difficulties faced by working-class women. Socialist women thought that women's emancipation should be seen as part of the struggle for socialism but could not agree on how much importance to give the vote. The suffragists amongst them argued that political equality would raise women's industrial and social status and would give them greater power to influence social reforms. Socialist women found it difficult to juggle between competing loyalties – to class, party and gender – but managed to make a significant contribution to the suffrage campaign. Encouraged by socialist rhetoric of equality women demanded political rights for themselves. They argued that if women did not have political equality they would be unable to take part in the struggle to achieve socialism or to influence the shape of the new socialist society.

Socialist groups were committed in principle to women's suffrage, but in practice they rarely gave priority to the question. At the Second International meeting in Stuttgart in 1907, however, a resolution was passed calling on members to 'struggle energetically' for women's suffrage as part of a broad demand for all men and women to have the vote. This caused tensions between socialists and women's suffrage groups in countries where the male franchise was a restricted one. In the latter suffragists called for votes for women on the same terms as men, or a limited franchise, even if this meant that only propertied or educated women would be enfranchised, since it was argued that the principle of removing a restriction based simply on sex was all important. Socialists on the other hand claimed that this would not benefit working-class women and called instead for adult suffrage, a demand that many suffragists feared could easily turn into support for manhood suffrage.

BOX 3.6

Suffrage demands

Limited suffrage

The call for votes for women on the same terms as men was described as a limited suffrage demand in countries where not all men were eligible to vote. In these circumstances only certain categories of women would have been enfranchised.

Universal or adult suffrage

The demand that all men and women over a certain age should be able to vote.

Manhood suffrage

The demand that all men over a certain age should be able to vote.
    The debates over which demand to put forward were affected by the extent to which the vote was linked to property ownership or tax paying status and the complicated relationship, therefore, to both sex and class.

Nonetheless, in countries such as Norway and Austria, it was socialist women who were instrumental in ensuring that franchise reforms that had given women the vote on a restricted basis were extended to include all women.

In Britain, the Independent Labour Party was unusual amongst European socialist parties in giving formal support at annual conferences to the demand for a limited suffrage. Many of its members were active in suffrage organizations and this pattern was repeated elsewhere in Europe. In Austria and Germany, however, it was the socialist women's organizations, the largest and most well-organized on the Continent, that took a leading role in the suffrage campaign. In Germany they campaigned vigorously in the pre-war years, organizing the first Proletarian Women's Day in 1911 when demonstrations in favour of women's suffrage were held throughout the country. Street marches, with women carrying placards and banners, provided a contrast to the moderate methods of the liberal feminist suffrage groups. Although there was hostility between socialist women and the 'bourgeois' women's movement the two groups did make links with each other, in particular at a local level.

At an international level there was a huge gulf between the IWSA, with its largely moderate, educated middle-class membership and the Socialist Women's International. Individual socialist women such as Isabella Ford from Britain and Martina Kramers from The Netherlands took an active part in the IWSA, but it is significant that neither of them were simultaneously heavily involved in the Socialist Women's International. Indeed, socialist women often found that suffrage organizations that were set up ostensibly to cater for the needs of all women were in fact run by educated, middle-class women who controlled the agenda and direction of the organizations. In 1913, for example, Martina Kramers was asked by Carrie Chapman Catt to give up her position as editor of the IWSA journal *Jus Sufragii* because of her private life (she lived with a married man) and her socialism.

Achievement of the vote

By 1920 women had gained the vote in most countries in Europe and North America. Suffragists in France and Italy had to wait until after the Second World War and it was not until 1971 that Switzerland finally conceded voting rights. What explains the timing of women's achievement of the vote and why did some governments resist women's demands for so long? The American states of the mid-West, New Zealand and Australia, where women were enfranchised earlier than elsewhere, were colonial farming societies with a preponderance of men who felt less threatened by women's enfranchisement than their counter-parts elsewhere (Grimshaw 1987). Religion could also play a part. In general, Catholic countries were more resistant to women's suffrage than Protestant ones. In France, for example, Republicans feared that women were controlled by parish priests and might wish to restore the monarchy and so they were wary of any demand for the vote. Similarly in Spain there was an emphasis on women's 'traditional' role in the family. When it was suggested that widows should be able to vote in municipal elections in 1908 this was opposed on the grounds that it would be like handing the vote over to the priest. And yet in Czechoslovakia, a predominantly Catholic country, the Czechs associated the Habsburgs with loyalty to Rome and supported women's suffrage as a way to strengthen the nationalist movement. In Ireland also the church did little to prevent the development of a strong, militant movement.

A long held assumption is that women achieved the vote as a reward for their war services, but this does not stand up to close scrutiny. In France and Italy women were not enfranchised, despite their efforts during the war, while in Britain politicians were reluctant at first to include women in proposals made in 1916 to extend the male franchise. When British women did achieve a measure of suffrage in 1918, it was restricted to those over 30 who had been far less involved in the war effort than younger women. Where the war did have an impact was in creating political and social upheavals that led to the development of new political systems. Thus women gained the vote in the liberal democratic governments created after the war, including Czechoslovakia, Austria, Hungary and Germany where it was assumed that women would support moderate governments against attack from both the left and the right.

What is clear is that no one single explanation will suffice, and that the achievement of the franchise must be understood within the complex political, religious and social context of individual countries. It is important though not to lose sight of women's agency and the extent to which they played an active role in their own emancipation. By itself, the existence of a strong suffrage movement was clearly not enough to guarantee success. In Switzerland, for example, women did not gain the vote until long after other western European countries, but there had been an active suffrage movement since the early twentieth century. Women also gained the vote relatively early in countries where the suffrage movement was weak or non-existent. Else-where, however, suffrage campaigning and the publicity generated did ensure that politicians were not able to ignore the demand for the vote. There was no guarantee, for example, that women in Britain would have been included in the 1918 Franchise Bill if they had not continued to lobby the government and to make their presence felt. They also maintained their pressure until an equal franchise was granted in 1928. Similarly in the United States it was women's hard work at a national and at a state level that ensured that the Senate would ratify the Nineteenth Amendment, giving women the vote, in 1920, albeit with the narrowest of margins.

The suffrage campaign was a key moment in the develop-ment of a feminist consciousness. Suffrage activists, organized in groups that were predominantly female, gained a heightened sense of solidarity with other women as they battled against hostile governments to achieve their aims. This could lead, as in the case of the WSPU, to an emphasis on the oppression of all women as a sex by men and an appeal to put gender loyalty above class and party. Although they were inspired by individual acts of courage, the emphasis was on women acting together and many suffrage campaigners gave a full-time commitment to the cause in the years immediately before the First World War. On the other hand, the suffrage movement revealed, and at times exacerbated, the differences between women. Suffrage groups were often hostile to each other and failed to agree on political strategies and on methods of action. At the IWSA meeting of 1906, for example, Millicent Fawcett challenged the credentials of Dora Montefiore, a member of the WSPU. Dora was only allowed to speak after the Dutch and Hungarian delegates wrote to the president asking that she should be heard on behalf of the 'insurgent women of England'. Suffrage groups had their own colours and slogans that reinforced a sense of identification with a particular group rather than to suffragists more generally. As the social and political backgrounds from which suffrage campaigners were drawn began to widen, tensions increased between them and the leaders of the movement who were still largely well educated, middle class and moderate in outlook. For those women who remained politically active once the vote was won differences could be exacerbated as they sought to pursue their feminism through mainstream political parties as well as through women's organizations. At the same time there was a growing tension between women's involvement in nationalism and anti-colonial struggles and the internationalism of the women's movement. These issues will be considered in the next chapter.

Further reading

For an overview of suffrage campaigns in different countries in the nineteenth and early twentieth centuries, see June Hannam, Mitzi Auchterlonie and Katherine Holden, *International Encyclopaedia of Women's Suffrage*, Santa Barbera, CA: ABC-Clio, 2000.

Comparative studies include: Richard J. Evans, *The Feminists: Women's Emancipation Movements in Europe, America and Australasia, 1840–1920*, London: Croom Helm, 1977; Karen Offen, *European Feminisms, 1780–1950: A Political History*, Stanford, CA: Stanford University Press, 2000; Gisela Bock, *Women in European History*, Oxford: Blackwell, 2002; and Caroline Daley and Melanie Nolan (eds) *Suffrage and Beyond: International Feminist Perspectives*, Auckland: University of Auckland Press, 1994.

There is a vast literature on the history of the suffrage movements in Britain and the United States. The subject is best
approached, therefore, through overview texts that provide a
guide to further reading, for example: Christine Bolt, *The
Women's Movements in the United States and Britain from the 1790s
to the 1920s*, Hemel Hempstead: Harvester Wheatsheaf, 1993;
Harold L. Smith, *The British Women's Suffrage Campaigns, 1866–
1928*, London: Addison Wesley Longman, 1998; Paula Bartley,
Votes for Women, London: Hodder, 1998. Elizabeth Crawford,
The Women's Suffrage Movement. A Reference Guide, London: UCL
Press, 1999, is an invaluable reference guide to all aspects of
the British suffrage movement. Other countries are covered by
the following: Steven C. Hause with Anne R. Kenney, *Women's
Suffrage and Social Politics in the French Third Republic*, Princeton,
NJ: Princeton University Press, 1984; Audrey Oldfield, *Woman
Suffrage in Australia. A Gift or a Struggle*, Cambridge: Cam-
bridge University Press, 1992; Patricia Grimshaw, *Women's
Suffrage in New Zealand*, Auckland: Auckland University Press,
1987; Ida Blom, 'The Struggle for Women's Suffrage in Norway,
1885–1913', *Scandinavian Journal of History*, 5, 1980; Katherine
David, 'Czech Feminists and Nationalism in the Late Habsburg
Monarchy: "The First in Austria"', *Journal of Women's History*, 3,
2, 1991; Linda H. Edmondson, *Feminism in Russia, 1900–1917*,
Stanford, CA: Stanford University Press, 1984; D. Dahlerup,
'Three Waves of Feminism in Denmark', in Gabrielle Griffin
and Rosie Braidotti (eds) *Thinking Differently: A Reader in Euro-
pean Women's Studies*, London: Zed Books, 2002; H. Anderson,
Utopian Feminism: Women's Movements in Fin-de-Siècle Vienna,
New Haven, CT: Yale University Press, 1992; and Werner
Thönnesen, *The Emancipation of Women: The Rise and Decline of*

the Women's Movement in German Social Democracy, 1863–1933, London: Pluto, 1976.

The complex relationship between ideas of equality and difference are explored in: Barbara Caine, *Victorian Feminists*, Oxford: Oxford University Press, 1992; and Jill Scott, 'Deconstructing Equality-Versus-Difference: Or the Uses of Post-Structuralist Theory for Feminism', *Feminist Studies*, 14, 1988. The ideas of individuals and groups are explored in: Jane Rendall, 'Citizenship, Culture and Civilisation: The Languages of British Suffragists, 1866–1874', in Daley and Nolan (eds) *Suffrage and Beyond*; Les Garner, *Stepping Stones to Women's Liberty: Feminist Ideas in the Women's Suffrage Movement, 1900–1918*, London: Heinemann, 1984; Susan K. Kent, *Sex and Suffrage in Britain, 1860–1914*, London: Routledge, 1990; and Gayle Gullett, *Becoming Citizens: The Emergence and Development of the California Women's Movement, 1880–1911*, Champagne: University of Illinois Press, 2000. The arguments of anti-suffrage women are discussed in Julia Bush, *Edwardian Ladies and Imperial Power*, London: Leicester University Press, 2000.

For an overview of the differences between 'imperial feminists', see Clare Midgley, 'White Women, "Race" and Empire', in June Purvis (ed.) *Women's History. Britain, 1850–1945*, London: UCL Press, 1995. Key texts for understanding the relationship between women's suffrage, colonialism and imperialism are: Antoinette Burton, *Burdens of History: British Feminists, Indian Women and Imperial Culture, 1865–1914*, Chapel Hill, NC: University of North Carolina Press, 1994; Barbara Ramusack, 'Cultural Missionaries, Maternal Imperialists, Feminist Allies: British Women Activists in India, 1865–1945', *Women's Studies International Forum*, 13, 2, 1990; Mineke Bosch, 'Colonial

Dimensions of Dutch Women's Suffrage; and Aletta Jacobs's Travel Letters from Africa and Asia, 1911–12, *Journal of Women's History*, 11, 2, 1999. The complexities of race are discussed in: Vron Ware, *Beyond The Pale. White Women. Racism and History*, London: Verso 1992; Marilyn Lake, 'The Ambiguities for Feminists of National Belonging: Race and Gender in the Imagined Australian Community', in Ida Blom, Karen Hagemann and Catherine Hall (eds) *Gendered Nations: Nationalism and Gender Order in the Long Nineteenth Century*, Oxford: Berg, 2000; Ian C. Fletcher, Laura E. Nym Mayhall and Philippa Levine (eds) *Women's Suffrage in the British Empire: Citizenship, Nation and Race*, London: Routledge, 2000; and Cherryl Walker, *The Women's Suffrage Movement in South Africa*, Cape Town: University of Cape Town, 1979.

The iconic status of Emmeline Pankhurst is explored in two recent biographies: Paula Bartley, *Emmeline Pankhurst*, London: Routledge, 2002; and June Purvis, *Emmeline Pankhurst: A Biography*, London: Routledge, 2002. Martin Pugh, *The Pankhursts*, Harmondsworth: Penguin, 2002 looks at the contribution of the family as a whole and the relationship between its members. Debates about the nature of militancy are considered in: Sandra S. Holton, 'Women and the Vote', in June Purvis (ed.) *Women's History. Britain, 1850–1945*, London: UCL Press, 1995; and Laura E. Nym Mayhall, *The Militant Suffrage Movement: Citizenship and Resistance in Britain, 1860–1930*, Oxford: Oxford University Press, 2003. Laura E. Nym Mayhall and Hilda Kean, 'Searching for the Present in Past Defeat: The Construction of Historical and Political identity in British Feminism in the 1920s and 30s', *Women's History Review*, 3, 1, 1994 consider the ways in which suffragettes writing in the inter-war years shaped later histories of militancy. A key text for understanding the imagery of the movement and the role that it played in suffrage politics is: Lisa Tickner, *The Spectacle of Women: Imagery of the Suffrage Campaign, 1907–1914*, London: Chatto and Windus, 1987. For propaganda, including plays, novels, poetry and advertising, see Margaret Finnegan, *Selling Suffrage: Consumer Culture and Votes for Women*, New York: Columbia University Press, 1999; Alice Sheppard, *Cartooning for Suffrage*, Albuquerque: University of New Mexico Press, 1994; and relevant essays in: Maroula Joannou and June Purvis (eds) *The Women's Suffrage Movement: New Feminist Perspectives*, Manchester: Manchester University Press, 1998.

A pioneering text on the involvement of working women and the relationship between socialism and suffrage is Jill Liddington and Jill Norris, *One Hand Tied Behind Us. The Rise of the Women's Suffrage Movement*, London: Virago, 1978. See also Ellen C. DuBois, 'Woman Suffrage Round the World: Three Phases of Internationalism', in Daley and Nolan (eds) *Suffrage and Beyond*, Auckland: Auckland University Press, 1994; Marilyn J. Boxer and Jean H. Quataert (eds) *Socialist Women: European Socialist Feminism in the Nineteenth and Twentieth Centuries*, New York: Elsevier, 1978; Richard J. Evans, *Comrades and Sisters: Feminism, Socialism and Pacifism in Europe, 1870– 1945*, Brighton: Harvester Wheatsheaf, 1987; and June Hannam and Karen Hunt, *Socialist Women. Britain, 1880s–1920s*, London: Routledge, 2001.

The debate on the impact of war is considered in Penny Summerfield, 'Women and War in the Twentieth Century', in Purvis (ed.) *Women's History* and in Bock, *Women in European History*.

Note

1   By 1914 the NUWSS had 380 affiliated societies with over
    53,000 members. The militant groups were smaller: the WFL
    had 4,000 members, while the WSPU had 88 branches in 1913,
    but its newspaper had a circulation of 30–40,000.

CHAPTER 4

Feminism, internationalism and nationalism in the twentieth century

LATIN AMERICA, the Caribbean, Asia and parts of the Middle East took centre stage in the inter-war years in the struggle for women's suffrage and women's rights. Feminists here were often involved in nationalist and anti-colonial struggles and had a complicated relationship with Western feminism. To what extent was it possible to link a nationalist with an internationalist consciousness and how does this affect our understanding of the term 'universal sisterhood' (Sinha, Guy and Woollacott 1998: 345, 350)?

After the upheavals of the First World War issues of race and the need for self-determination came to the fore. Within the British Empire India demanded a larger degree of self-government, while countries in Latin America expressed nationalist and anti-imperialist sentiments when the United States increased its military and economic presence. The Russian and Mexican revolutions also inspired many to seek a far-reaching transformation of economic and social structures. In this uncertain time women increasingly tried to make their voices heard and demanded change in all areas of their lives, including the right to vote.

Latin America, the Caribbean and women's suffrage

Feminist campaigns gathered momentum in the inter-war years in Latin America and parts of the Caribbean. Women had already begun to organize together to demand reforms in the early 1900s. It was in the 1920s and 30s, however, that organized women's groups in Argentina, Uruguay, Brazil, Chile and Mexico expanded in number and gained greater publicity. The characteristics of these groups varied a great deal from country to country – so much so that Latin America can be described as a site of 'competing feminisms' (Ehrick 1998: 415). Brazil and Uruguay, for instance, had very different suffrage campaigns although women were enfranchised in both countries in 1932. The suffrage movement in Brazil was unusual since it was led by a small group of upper and middle-class urban women, with close ties to the country's political elite, who used their influence with members of the government as a way to achieve their aims. In an attempt to mobilize more women, however, they did expand their activities to include letter campaigns, press releases and petitions. They were inspired by developments in Europe and some, including Bertha Lutz, had personal friendship links with women in the International Woman Suffrage Alliance. In Uruguay, where the church was weak, the women's movement followed a liberal feminist pattern that was familiar in Europe. Women's organizations, including the Uruguayan National Council of Women (1916) and the Uruguay Alliance of Women for Suffrage (1919) were established. Led by a doctor, Paulina Luisi, they drew their members initially from the educated and professional middle class but then sought to expand their membership base by appealing to literate working-class women.

Feminists argued about aims, priorities and tactics and often shifted their position over time. Equality for women in education, the family and the law was a key objective for all of them, but the vote, and the basis on which to demand the franchise, was far more contentious. Class differences were especially important. In Puerto Rico, for example, it was working women from the trade union movement who, in 1908, first lobbied for a bill to give women all the rights enjoyed by men under the law. From this point on both working and upper-class women gave priority to the suffrage. But they campaigned from separate platforms and could not agree about whether to ask for a limited or a universal franchise. In Mexico too class proved to be divisive. In the 1920s working-class and peasant women formed groups associated with trade unions or the Communist Party and were concerned with economic questions, while urban middle-class women concentrated on the vote. In the mid-1930s, however, they joined together in an umbrella group, the Sole Front for Women's Rights. This gave priority to women's suffrage and at its peak had 50,000 members organized in 800 societies, although women did not gain the vote until 1958.

The suffrage might have proved elusive in the 1920s, but feminists did manage to achieve many civil rights for women – in Argentina, for example, the Civil Code was revised in 1926.

BOX 4.1

Civil rights

The legal rights that women gained in areas such as employment, education and the family (including divorce, custody of children and ownership of property) are referred to as civil rights. This can be contrasted with political rights, in particular the right to vote.

In some countries Civil Law Codes could be used to reinforce male power over women. The Napoleonic Code of 1804 gave the husband full legal power over his wife, her property and her children. First promulgated in France the Code was influential throughout Europe in the nineteenth century.

In the period 1929 to the mid-1930s, however, the vote was gained in a number of countries, including Ecuador, Uruguay, Brazil and Cuba. Women's enfranchisement was closely linked to the interests of the mainstream political parties. In Uruguay members of the government became more sympathetic to women's suffrage once they were convinced that women would be a force for stability rather than being associated with socialism or anarchism, while in Brazil and Cuba suffragists benefited from the introduction of liberal and reforming governments who sought their support. Viewed either as reactionary conservatives or as dangerous radicals, women found themselves in a contradictory position. Sometimes this helped, and at other times it hindered, their campaign for the vote. For example, the deeply conservative pro-Catholic country of Ecuador was the first to enfranchise women in Latin America in 1929, albeit on a limited basis. The ruling coalition faced a threat from socialists and saw women as compliant and loyal to the status quo. In Mexico, however, women's association with conservatism worked against them. Congress refused to ratify a suffrage amendment to the constitution in 1939 because it was feared that women would support the conservative opposition party.

Women did not gain the vote in the other major countries in the region, including Argentina, Bolivia, Peru, Nicaragua and Mexico until after the Second World War.[1] A liberal political climate again proved to be important. In Costa Rica, for example, women were finally able to vote and stand for election in 1949 after the Partido Liberación Nacional had come to power and the Assembly of Representatives had drafted a new constitution. In Argentina it was the election of General Perón as president that was to lead to women's suffrage in 1947 after his wife, Eva, mobilized the support of working-class women. Nonetheless, feminists opposed many of the arguments that she used, in particular the assertion that political participation would make women more attractive.

Women's suffrage in India and Egypt

Nationalist and anti-colonial struggles provided the context for women to raise their own demands in countries subject to formal colonial rule, including India, Egypt, Tunisia and Syria. Educated upper and middle-class women, influenced both by the European women's movement and by nationalism, took the lead. In India, for example, Sarojini Naidu was a key figure.

In 1917 Naidu led an all-India women's delegation to ask the Montagu-Chelmsford Committee on constitutional reform to enfranchise Indian women on the same terms as men. This was not accepted, but women's protests did lead to the

BOX 4.2

Sarojini Naidu, 1879–1949

Sarojini Chattopadhyaya was born in Hyderabad, India, into a Brahmin family. She was educated in England at King's College, London and Girton College Cambridge and in 1898 married a doctor, G.R. Naidu. She was involved in nationalist politics before the First World War and also took up the cause of women, addressing a meeting of the British Dominions Woman Suffrage Movement in London in 1914 on the topic of the 'ideals of Indian Womanhood'. Throughout the inter-war years she continued to pursue the two causes of Indian independence and women's rights and demanded that all women, regardless of their religious affiliation, should be able to vote. In 1925 she became the second woman president of the Indian National Congress and in 1931 was the official representative of Indian women's organizations at the Round table Conference in London.

concession that women who possessed the requisite educational and property qualifications could vote for representatives to provincial legislatures. Although there were times when women were expected to put the cause of Indian independence before women's rights, they continued to campaign for a variety of reforms, including the suffrage for all Indian women.

In a volatile political situation feminists often had to change the nature of their demands and to shift their priorities. In Egypt, for example, women took part in the uprising against the British in 1919 but felt completely let down when, after independence in 1922, the suffrage was restricted to men. In 1923, therefore, Hudá Sha'rawi founded the Egyptian Feminist Union to campaign for a range of reforms, including political rights.

BOX 4.3

Hudá Sha'rawi, 1879–1947

Sha'rawi was the most influential figure in the inter-war feminist movement in Egypt. The daughter of a wealthy landowner and provincial administrator, she was married at the age of 13 to 'Ali Sha'rawi who was prominent in the Wafd, the Egyptian Nationalist Party. Hudá was expected to help her husband in 1919 by organizing resistance to British rule and she became first president of the Ladies Central Committee of the Wafd Party. In 1923, after the declaration of Egyptian independence and her husband's death, she formed the Egyptian Feminist Union to fight for women's rights. Sha'rawi took an active part in the International Woman Suffrage Alliance and developed friendships with her counterparts in Europe and North America. By the 1940s the upper-class EFU was losing its dominance in Egyptian feminism but, through her energetic leadership, Sha'rawi had helped to keep the suffrage question alive during the inter-war years. Women were finally enfranchised in 1956, several years after her death.

It was not easy to maintain a commitment to political rights. Nationalists increasingly emphasized women's social role rather than their individual rights and so the EFU gave greater attention to women's education and the reform of the personal status law. There was some success for this tactic in the 1920s; equal secondary school education for girls, the entry of women into the state university and the raising of the minimum marriage age for both sexes were all introduced.

The political climate changed in 1934 with a return to liberalism. In the same year the IWSA held its congress in neighbouring Istanbul and women gained the suffrage in Turkey.

This gave a new impetus to the suffrage campaign in Egypt and the EFU demanded votes for educated women. In the late 1930s, however, the Palestine question dominated politics for men and women and it was not until towards the end of the Second World War that a more sustained attempt was made to raise the issue of women's political rights. Sha'rawi spoke eloquently at the Arab Women's Congress in Cairo in 1944 in favour of political rights for all Arab women. Two other suffrage groups that aimed to attract a broader middle-class membership now joined the EFU in its campaign. One of the leaders, Doria Shafik, employed militant methods. She led an invasion by 1,500 women of the Egyptian parliament in 1951 and was one of eight women who went on hunger strike three years later. Shafik's arguments, emphasizing the freedom of the individual and a secular approach, was in the tradition of liberal feminism and she was placed under house arrest by President Nasser in 1957. A younger generation of university students linked women's liberation with socialism and communism, but in a context of increasing nationalist pressure to expel British troops from Egypt feminists joined forces with fundamentalist women in a common nationalist cause. The pressure of suffrage campaigners, combined with the needs of a modernizing state, did lead Nasser to introduce votes for women in 1956, but women still had to make a special request to register their votes.

Feminism, nationalism and anti-colonialism

When feminists took part in mixed-sex politics they were often torn in their loyalties. What should come first – loyalty to their sex, or their party or their class? Or was it likely to be more complicated than that? There was usually a balancing act at any one time as priorities and tactics shifted. This could mean that feminists had differing views about what was meant by women's emancipation and how best to achieve it in specific political contexts. In China, for example, Xiang Jingyu, leader of the women's section of the Communist Party in the 1920s, argued that the vote was irrelevant to women under the current social system and urged them to join with working men to overthrow imperial rule which would then be a prerequisite for the suffrage. Similarly in Chile, liberal feminists refrained from campaigning for the vote in the 1920s because they feared the influence of the Catholic Church among women. Teachers attending feminist congresses in Mexico viewed the vote with suspicion since they believed that women should not become involved with corrupt masculine regimes.

In some instances, as in Sierra Leone and Ghana in the 1950s, women found it difficult to make their voices heard in nationalist, anti-colonial and revolutionary struggles and suppressed their own demand for political equality in order to give priority to other struggles. In contrast, in Vietnam, the Communist Party emphasized the importance of women's participation in politics in order to strengthen the revolutionary movement in 1937 and 1938. Party branches formed women's committees and at a May Day rally in Hanoi in 1938 thousands of women marched through the streets. In her speech to the rally Bao Tam demanded the 'progressive eradication of barriers differentiating men and women' (Jayawardena 1986: 210).

It was common for individual women to shift their political positions over time. Domínguez Navarro, a Cuban lawyer from a lower-middle-class background, provides a good example of this. She was involved in the feminist movement and then became increasingly drawn to revolutionary politics. In the late 1920s she joined other politically active women in opposing Machado's dictatorship and in 1928 left the Cuban Feminist National Alliance to form the Women's Labour Union that had links with the Communist Party. During a second term in prison she wrote that the feminist movement 'with its political and civic aspirations now seems to me too narrow a mould within which to struggle . . .' Ehrick makes the interesting point that whereas liberal feminists thought that a concern with class or nationalist politics was a less progressive position, 'now we see a Cuban feminist coming to the conclusion that it is being solely concerned with women's issues which is confining and backward, and that the incorporation of class issues was what the historical moment required' (Ehrick 1998: 416).

Indeed, contemporaries often equated nationalism with progress since it highlighted questions of citizenship and political representation that could be seen as part of a modernizing agenda. It is not surprising that feminists also looked at women's suffrage in this light. In countries such as New Zealand and Australia the early enfranchisement of women was viewed with some pride as an indicator of civilization and of the progress that these young nations had achieved. In India too feminists expressed pride that the provincial legislatures had unanimously agreed to remove the sex disqualification for the vote. One suffragist Mrinalini Sen claimed that 'while in the European countries women had to struggle hard for the attainment of their political rights women of India experience no difficulty in securing the same' (Sinha 2000: 231).

Feminists used a variety of arguments to justify their demands for greater public influence. Where cultural and religious values reinforced women's identification with the home, and male authority within the household, as in Latin America, feminists linked together nationalism, women's role as mothers and women's suffrage. They argued that if women realized the connection between home and the public world they would try to influence collective action, in particular the achievement of social reforms to solve social problems, and that this would ensure the development of the nation as well as civic rights for women (Lavrin 1995). In Syria and Lebanon, on the other hand, feminists avoided controversial questions such as the vote in the 1930s in the hope that they would gain support for other social reforms affecting women's social position. They praised domestic work and philanthropy as a national service and called for social rather than political rights to be able to carry out this task. It was

---

BOX 4.4

Patriotic motherhood

It was frequently suggested that women, as mothers and educators of their children, could play a vital role in forging a sense of national identity and patriotism. Thus they could play a role as active citizens without having the vote. The notion was first developed during the French Revolution and became an important feature of liberal nationalist movements in Europe in the nineteenth century and of nationalist and anti-colonial movements in the inter-war years. Although it was an argument associated with anti suffragists, feminists could also use their 'patriotic' role to demand political rights.

a tactic designed to broaden the appeal of women's organizations, to mobilize mothers and to give them an influence in the growing movement for independence from France (Thompson 2000). This form of 'patriotic motherhood' has echoes of the 'republican' and 'patriotic' motherhood that was a feature of nineteenth-century nationalist movements in Europe.

In countries subject to colonial rule, in particular where Islam was the predominant religion, feminist arguments and demands had to be developed in a context in which many nationalist and religious leaders sought to distance themselves from the West. Thus, respect for women's traditional roles in Muslim families and support for practices such as veiling were seen as a rejection of the influence of the colonial power. In Algeria 'women found themselves trapped by a conservative vision of their role in society justified by anti-colonialism' (Gadant 1995: 122). Two competing feminist arguments can be identified. One took a secularist approach to politics and looked to the West as representing progress. Its upper-class adherents had usually been educated in Europe and had friendship links with European feminists. Hudá Sha'rawi and Saiza Nabarawi, for example, were closely associated with the IWSA and, after attending its congress in Rome in 1923, removed their veils when they returned to Egypt. Although Shar'awi was a nationalist who opposed British domination, she accepted many Western ideas and argued that there should be gradual reforms towards adopting Western institutions and a secularist understanding of the state. The other feminist argument sought to affirm women's sense of self within Islam and to see it as part of a renovation of the whole society. This was expressed by the writer Malak Nassef who opposed unveiling, arguing that those who unveiled were upper-class women who were not motivated by a desire for liberty or the pursuit of knowledge, but were obsessed by fashion. Her views on veiling were, however, complex, since she was critical of men who sought to impose their own views on the subject onto women. She argued 'we must be wary of man being as despotic about liberating us as he has been about our enslavement' (Ahmed 1992: 182). Although Sha'rawi's brand of feminism, which looked to the West, was the most prominent perspective during the period, those who campaigned for women and the nation in Islamist terms became more potent in the latter decades of the twentieth century.

Internationalism and 'universal sisterhood'

Did these national tensions, in particular between those subject to colonial rule and women in Western societies, undermine the notion that there could be a 'universal sisterhood' that crossed national boundaries? The suffrage campaign, in particular, did encourage women to see themselves as part of an international movement. As already noted in Chapter 3, formal links were made through the establishment of transnational organizations before the First World War, including the International Council of Women and the International Woman Suffrage Alliance.

Women met regularly at international meetings and forged strong friendships. They kept in touch by writing copious letters which encouraged feelings of solidarity and enabled them to deepen personal relationships. For example, the American Carrie Chapman Catt, the Dutch suffragists Aletta Jacobs and Rosa Manus and the Hungarian Rosika Schwimmer were particularly close friends. At first friendships tended to be between women

BOX 4.5

International Woman Suffrage Alliance

Founded in Berlin in 1904, the IWSA aimed to promote women's suffrage in individual countries and to encourage suffragists to see themselves as part of an international movement. It also acted as a central bureau to collect and disseminate information. By 1913 there were 26 national affiliates, largely from Europe, North America and Australia. International congresses were held every two years until the outbreak of war. In the inter-war years the list of national affiliates grew to 51, including Egypt, India, Japan and countries in Latin America. Those who already had the suffrage took up other campaigns, particularly peace. In 1926, therefore, the IWSA took the new name of International Alliance of Women for Suffrage and Equal Citizenship and in 1946 became the International Alliance of Women. The programme of the IAW was peace, democracy, women's rights and support for the United Nations.

in the United States and Europe, but by the inter-war years Bertha Lutz from Brazil and the Egyptian feminist leaders Hudá Sha'rawi and Doria Shafik, among others, were included in these networks.

Familial language was used by women to express their connections with each other. Bertha Lutz, for example, addressed Carrie Chapman Catt as 'my dear mother Mrs Catt' and signed herself as Catt's Brazilian daughter. This could imply that feminists were challenging the view that 'the only families were national families' (Rupp 1997: 199) but familial terms could also reinforce power relationships between women based on age and nationality. European feminist leaders, for instance, figure prominently in the autobiographies and memoirs of Egyptian suffragists, although this is not the case the other way round (Badran 1995).

Some women were inveterate travellers and used their visits to other countries to propagandize for the suffrage. Mary Leavitt, the United States envoy of the Woman's Christian Temperance Union, travelled throughout the world and left behind 86 women's organizations that aimed to get the vote. Women from Australia and New Zealand, who already had the vote, were welcomed as speakers in the imperial heartland. In 1911, for example, the Women's Social and Political Union invited the Australian Vida Goldstein to address numerous meetings in Britain in order to encourage suffrage campaigners facing strong resistance. She met all the main suffrage leaders and offered them advice and support, but also found that her experience of the militant campaign affected many of her own ideas, in particular over the extent to which male and female socialists could cooperate together in a common struggle.

The ability to travel was largely restricted to women who had resources and leisure time and therefore women active in international organizations were predominantly from middle-class or upper-class backgrounds. They shared the assumptions of their class and generation that the West signified progress and civilization, in particular, in relation to the position of women, and therefore it was part of their role to stimulate suffrage activity elsewhere. Nonetheless, feminists from the United States and western Europe could also find their own preconceptions challenged when they travelled widely. British suffragists, for example, were surprised to find Iranian women making demands for the vote in their country's constitutional crisis of 1906–11, while the suffrage movement was still at its height in Britain. Similarly, when Carrie Chapman Catt went on a world tour with Aletta Jacobs in 1911–12 she had not expected to find that women in Burma had the right to own property, engage in business and vote in municipal elections and, therefore, in many respects were better off than women in the West. And yet at the same time that she made this observation she also noted 'the languor of people in such sunshine' and the fact that in the Orient women were often held in 'most pitiful tutelage, and denied every vestige of personal liberty' (Rupp 1997: 76–7).

Tensions within the IWSA

Was it possible for feminists from across the world to share common interests despite their national differences? Trans-national groups took pride in the international flavour of their proceedings and argued that women, as the guardians and nurturers of life, were committed to peace and international understanding. They believed that they could talk across their differences and achieve a broad unity of purpose, but this was difficult to sustain. The ICW and IWSA were dominated by well-educated upper- and middle-class Christian women of European origins who displayed national pride through cultural symbols such as national costume and dance. There were immediate conflicts with socialists, many of whom chose to pursue the fight for women's right to vote from within their own organization, the Socialist Women's International. In the inter-war years further conflicts arose as women from outside Europe and North America demanded that their voices and perspectives be heard.

The First World War gave an impetus to international feminist activities as women from many nations joined together in the Women's International League (WIL) to campaign for a peace by negotiation. Those who gained the vote in the aftermath of war then expanded their activities across a broad front. In the 1920s they sought to increase women's influence in the League of Nations, and to be a force for peace and disarmament. In 1919 the WIL changed its name to the Women's International League for Peace and Freedom, established a headquarters in Geneva and reaffirmed its aims of achieving peace and women's emancipation. It was the only women's organization that set policy at an international level and expected the national sections to follow its lead. WILPF, the International Council of Women and the IWSA campaigned for a range of other reforms, including educational opportunities, marital law reform and a change in the laws governing nationality for women who married someone from a different country.

Tensions, however, increased between the feminist movements of different countries. In the IWSA those who were still excluded from the franchise wanted to concentrate on women's suffrage, whereas those who had already gained the vote sought to widen the range of their activities to encompass peace and social reform. This raised fears that the issue of equal rights would be lost from view. It was agreed that the IWSA should continue to campaign for the suffrage. However, instead of women campaigning together against their common exclusion from political rights there was now a situation in which some women, mainly from Europe and North America, were working for the rights of others. This reinforced the assumption that in the West women were modern, educated and in control of their own lives and bodies in contrast to those in Arab countries or in colonial contexts who were not (Woollacott 1998).

Feminists in colonial contexts began to assert their own distinctive voices as their countries sought greater independence and self-determination. Indian women, for example, challenged the right of newly enfranchised British women to speak for them on the Commission, established in 1927, to recommend future political reforms in India. They demanded their own place on the Commission and clashed with the dominant British women's organizations over the nature of the proposals that were made to extend Indian women's franchise (Sinha 2000).

The views of the IWSA leadership were also increasingly criticized in the inter-war years. Hudá Sha'rawi, who was elected vice-president of the IWSA in 1923, voiced the concerns of the Muslim women of Palestine against Jewish immigration and challenged the Christian assumptions that lay behind the Alliance. Others sought to move away from the influence of the IWSA and to develop their own international links that would give them greater autonomy. In Uruguay, Mexico, Brazil and Argentina, suffragists built on friendship links that they had already made in congresses held in South America before the First World War. They carried out an extensive correspondence in which they began to develop their own methods and political strategies. Women from outside Europe and North America also travelled extensively and exerted an influence on each other. For instance Sarojini Naidu of the Indian National Congress inspired Sri Lankan middle-class women to demand the vote when she visited their country in 1922.

New organizations were formed that challenged the dominance of the IWSA and WILPF. The Pan-American Association for the Advancement of Women, established in 1922 sought a wide range of reforms, including women's suffrage, and aimed to improve communications among all American countries and to exert an influence on policy within the region. Feminists in the Americas were able to work together for a number of common goals, but the dominance of the United States caused discontent. The American Carrie Chapman Catt who had founded the Association was looked on with suspicion because of her self-proclaimed missionary role to countries where feminist movements were less well developed. Feminists in South America, therefore, asserted their independence by joining with their Iberian counterparts to form the International League of Iberian and Hispanic American Women. Tensions were, though, also present within Latin America itself. Feminists from Uruguay sought to link with their counterparts in Chile, Cuba and Mexico, but they were suspicious of Argentina and feared that their own nation could be threatened as much by their close neighbours as by the United States.

Feminism and citizenship

In the inter-war years ties binding the constituent parts of the British Empire began to loosen. The self-governing Dominions, including Canada, Australia and New Zealand began to build distinct national identities for themselves within the new Commonwealth. Feminists wanted to ensure that they would have an influence over this process and raised their own issues, such as the nationality of married women and maintenance payments to deserted wives, in London and in Dominion capitals. Now that Australia and New Zealand were represented in their own right at the League of Nations women were aware that their citizenship status within the Empire had changed and they set out with a new sense of confidence to influence the shape of 'imperial feminism'. The first step was to form new organizations – the British Commonwealth League (BCL) and the Pan-Pacific Women's Association (PPWA) – to bring women together from across the Empire, the Commonwealth and the Pacific Rim to discuss issues that affected them all. This helped to shift the focus and perspectives of feminist campaigning away from the heartland of Europe.

The PPWA, for instance, sought to inform European based groups about the conditions of women's lives in Pacific Rim countries and in many respects encouraged women from India, Japan and the Philippines to speak for themselves. On the other hand, Angela Woollacott, a leading historian in the field, argues persuasively that PPWA members from Australia and New Zealand saw themselves as 'protecting less forward races' while in the BCL white women who could vote thought that it was their responsibility to look after the interests of native peoples. She suggests, therefore, that they substituted a new brand of 'Commonwealth feminism' for the older-style Imperial feminism (Woollacott 1998).

In the inter-war years, therefore, feminism was fractured in multiple ways – national, class, religious and racial differences could all undermine solidarity. On the other hand, feminists also sought to work together internationally and spoke a language of universal sisterhood. This could be seen as an example of the difficulties involved in creating a politics around the category 'woman', but in practice the situation was far more complex. Many feminists had a modest goal of working together over specific issues while accepting limitations to the notion of universal sisterhood. Nationalism and internationalism, for example, were not necessarily mutually exclusive concepts and it was possible to find space within them to build notions of 'sisterhood' and female solidarity. For the Dutch feminist Aletta Jacobs, for instance, internationalism was an intrinsic part of her national and imperial identity and was not something separate from it. Too small to rule their empire by force the Dutch claimed that they sought to foster international cooperation and peace while at the same time respecting local customs (Bosch 1999). On her travels in Africa and Asia, 1911–12, Jacobs expressed national pride in this outlook, which was compared favourably with the British attempt to 'civilize' the indigenous population. She then drew upon this concept of nationalism to support her international work as a member of the IWSA and as an organizer of the Women's Peace Congress at The Hague in 1915.

Feminists active in North American and European based international organizations such as the IWSA tended to view their demands for suffrage or for peace as universal issues, transcending differences between women. They were critical of feminists in Asia and the Middle East for being too 'nationalist' in their politics, but, as Leila Rupp points out in her path-breaking study of transnational women's organizations, that was only because they took their own nationalist interests for granted (Rupp 1998). If looked at from the perspective of women elsewhere then internationalism has a different meaning but could still encompass the concept of a universal sisterhood. Indian women, for instance, developed complex arguments about nationalism, colonialism and feminism. Although they were deeply engaged in the nationalist movement for independence from British rule, Indian feminists were also internationalist in outlook. Nonetheless, they had their own ideas about the meaning of feminist internationalism and objected when newly enfranchised British feminists assumed that they could speak for Indian women. They drew attention within organizations such as the IWSA and WILPF to the problems posed by European imperialism for notions of international solidarity while simultaneously developing their ideas in meetings outside European influence, such as the first All Asian Women's Conference held in Lahore in 1931 (Sinha 2000). Indian feminists thought that it would be possible to create a universal sisterhood but only if British feminists recognized their own failure to live up to this ideal. Thus they noted that British feminists, rather than supporting Indian women's demand for an equal franchise, took the same line as the British government in calling for a qualified franchise for women in India.

After the First World War organized feminist movements began to grow in strength outside Europe and North America. They developed in a context of nationalist and anti-colonial movements that sought greater independence and autonomy from Imperial rule, but feminists still asserted the right to speak for themselves. They challenged the colonial and racial assumptions of their counterparts in Europe and North America while also contesting attitudes about women's social role held by many male political and religious leaders in their own countries. Although they often appeared to put nationalism before other causes, feminists did pursue the interests of women and sought a role for themselves in building a national identity. At the same time they also made links with women from other countries and aimed to develop their own version of a 'universal sisterhood'.

A focus on these struggles provides a new lens through which to view the history of feminism. It reveals the rich variety of different feminisms and reinforces the argument that we should be wary of assuming that only certain aims, objectives and strategies deserve the label feminist. Despite differences in national cultures, as well as divisions based on class, race and political beliefs, in certain contexts women still expressed solidarity with each other on the grounds of a shared oppression as women.

Further reading

Important comparative studies of the women's movement in South America are: Asunción Lavrin, *Women, Feminism and Social Change in Argentina, Chile and Uruguay, 1890–1940*, Lincoln: University of Nebraska Press, 1995; and Christine Ehrick, ' "Madrinas and Missionaries": Uruguay and the Pan-American Women's Movement', *Gender and History*, 10, 3, 1998. For individual countries, see June Hahner, *Emancipating the Female Sex: The Struggle for Women's Rights in Brazil, 1850–1940*, Durham, NC: Duke University Press, 1990; Yamila Azize-Vargas, 'The Emergence of Feminism in Puerto Rico, 1870–1930', in Vikki L. Ruiz and Ellen C. DuBois (eds) *Unequal Sisters: A Multicultural Reader in US Women's History*, 3rd edn, London: Routledge, 2000; Anna Macías, *Against All Odds: The Feminist Movement in Mexico to 1940*, Westport, CT: Greenwood Press, 1982; and Manifran Carlson, *Feminismó! The Women's Movement in Argentina from its Beginnings to Eva Perón*, Chicago: Academy Chicago Publishers, 1988.

The relationship between nationalism, internationalism and feminism in the inter-war period is the subject of an important special issue of *Gender and History*, 10, 3, 1998. The debates are explored in the introduction written by the editors: Mrinalini Sinha, Donna J. Guy and Angela Woollacott, 'Introduction: Why Feminisms and Internationalism?'. Kumari Jayawardena, *Feminism and Nationalism in the Third World*, London: Zed Books, 1986 provides a comparison of several countries in Asia. The complicated relationship between Islam and women's rights, in particular the relationship between Westernization and feminism, is explored in: Margot Badran, *Feminists, Islam and Nation: Gender and the Making of Modern Egypt*, Princeton, NJ: Princeton University Press, 1995; and Leila Ahmed, *Women and Gender in Islam*, New Haven, CT: Yale University Press, 1992.

The informal friendship links between women at an international level are discussed in Mineke Bosch with Annemarie Kloosterman (eds) *Politics and Friendship: Letters from the International Woman Suffrage Alliance, 1902–1942*, Columbus, OH: Columbus University Press, 1990. The most comprehensive recent study of international women's organizations formed in Europe and North America is Leila Rupp, *Worlds of Women: The Making of an International Women's Movement*, Princeton, NJ: Princeton University Press, 1997. See also Leila Rupp, 'Feminisms and Internationalism: A View from the Centre', *Gender and History*, 10, 3, 1998. Bosch argues that the IWSA used exaggerated images of difference to point up the essential unity of women, whereas Rupp is interested to see how women with conflicting ideas could talk across their differences. For international organizations outside Europe, see Ehrick, 'Madrinas and Missionaries' and Angela Woollacott, 'Inventing Commonwealth and Pan-Pacific Feminisms: Australian Women's Internationalist Activism in the 1920s–30s', *Gender and History*, 10, 3, 1998.

Woollacott has a critical view of Australian feminists whereas Marilyn Lake suggests that their concern with Aboriginal women led them to recognize their country's racism.

The complicated relationship between feminists in colonial countries and their counterparts in the 'Imperial heartland' has been the subject of extensive research in recent years. Ian C. Fletcher, Laura E. Nym Mayhall and Philippa Levine (eds) *Women's Suffrage in the British Empire: Citizenship, Nation and Race*, London: Routledge, 2000 is an important and stimulating collection of essays. See also Elizabeth Thompson, *Colonial Citizens: Republican Rights, Paternal Privilege and Gender in French Syria and Lebanon*, New York: Columbia University Press, 2000.

Note

1 Women's suffrage was achieved in the following years: Argentina, 1947; Bolivia, 1953; Peru, 1955; Nicaragua, 1955; Mexico, 1958.

CHAPTER 5

Citizenship in North America and Europe in the inter-war years

AFTER CAMPAIGNING FOR SO LONG TO ACHIEVE THE VOTE, feminists now had to decide how to move forward from their new position as 'active citizens'. What goals and strategies should they adopt? Could they agree on a common outlook and act together? What kind of women's emancipation did they want to see? In comparison to the flamboyant and highly visible pre-war suffrage campaign, the women's movement in the inter-war years seemed more fragmented and to have less influence. The First World War had raised expectations that women's 'traditional' social roles could change, but once the conflict was over there was a desire to get back to 'normal' as quickly as possible. Domesticity and motherhood were emphasized as essential for the good of the family and of the state. Economic depression, high unemployment and fears about the quality and quantity of the population reinforced the assumption that women should devote their energies to family life, as did the development of conservative and fascist regimes that were explicitly anti-feminist in outlook.

War had encouraged the view that men and women, with their complementary roles, could work together for a common goal. It is hardly surprising, therefore, that individuals and organizations were reluctant to describe themselves as feminists, a label associated with a radical upheaval in family life and conflict between the sexes. Generation played a key role here. Young women had enjoyed greater personal freedoms during the War and tended to view feminist organizations as dull and old-fashioned. Former suffrage campaigners, therefore, complained that the young were only interested in personal fulfilment and pleasing men.

Political representation

In this context it was difficult for feminists to make an impact on politics, either as individuals or collectively. Only a few women were elected to representative assemblies. In Norway women never held more than 2.5% of seats on local councils in the inter-war years and gained only 3 out of the 150 seats in the Storting, the national parliament. In Austria eight women were elected to a Constituent Assembly of 170 deputies in 1919 and ten to the National Assembly in 1920. South Australia did not elect its first woman to parliament until 1959 and in Britain women comprised only a handful of MPs until the 1990s. Throughout the world women had to wait until the last two decades of the twentieth century before their representation on elected bodies showed any substantial increase. Embarking on a political career was not an easy option for women. Working practices in male-dominated representative assemblies made it difficult to combine a career with family life and women were reluctant to put themselves forward as candidates in a context in which national politics was still identified with masculinity. When they did seek to become candidates they found that the established political parties were unwilling to support the adoption of women as candidates in seats that could be won. Many of those who *were* successful in being elected did not adopt a feminist perspective or else found it difficult to work together because of conflicting party loyalties. In Germany, for example, where they comprised 10% of the Reichstag deputies in the 1920s, socialist and Catholic women disagreed about married women's employment and protection for unmarried mothers, although they cooperated on maternity benefits and protective legislation for women at the workplace.

How far, therefore, did women's social, economic and legal status improve after their enfranchisement? Legislation that enhanced their civil status was introduced in many countries while social welfare benefits such as family allowances and maternity pay provided economic support for married women. In Sweden, for example, married women obtained full legal equality in 1920 while in Britain the 1919 Sex Disqualification (Removal) Act provided for women to be admitted to the legal profession, to be eligible for jury service and to enter the civil service. In the new constitutions drawn up for the Weimar Republic in 1919 and the Irish Free State in 1922 it was declared that all citizens were equal under the law regardless of sex.

There was no guarantee, however, that legal equality would be put into practice, in particular when governments were anxious to reinforce male authority in the family. A strong, united feminist movement might have made a difference but this was largely absent. In Ireland for example, when the suffrage movement disintegrated, women no longer had an independent voice and found it difficult to resist new legislation designed to emphasize women's domesticity. In 1935, after pressure from the Catholic Church, legislation was introduced to restrict women's employment outside the home and in 1937 the constitution was re-written. Feminists managed to resist attempts to remove the clause 'without distinction of sex', but new articles were added that emphasized women's importance to the state as mothers and homemakers. This example provides a useful reminder that the gains women made could also be lost. In Hungary, for instance, women received the vote on equal terms with men in 1919, but were disenfranchised when the conservative wing of the nationalist movement came to power. After 1921 the vote was restricted to women over 30 who fulfilled educational and economic qualifications and full suffrage was not regained until 1945. In Spain women were successful in their campaign to ensure that the new constitution of the Second Republic, ratified in 1931, would include women's enfranchisement. There was fear among liberals that women would be a force for conservatism, but socialists and Catholics supported the measure. Clara Campoamor of the Radical Party was a particularly influential voice in the debate, arguing that Spain should provide an example of the best, most modern form of democracy.

The Republic also introduced other reforms that benefited women, including a secularized marriage law, civil divorce and the end of regulated prostitution. When Franco came to power in 1936, however, women were disenfranchised and emphasis was

BOX 5.1

Clara Rodríguez Campoamor

Clara Campoamor was a leading feminist in Spain in the early twentieth century and was instrumental in ensuring women gained the vote in 1931. Born into a poor family in Madrid in 1888, she had to go out to work at the age of 13 but studied part time and eventually gained a degree in law in 1924. She joined the National Association of Spanish Women, a group dedicated to obtaining political rights for women and, with the fall of the Spanish dictator Rivera in 1930, she threw herself into radical and socialist politics. As a member of the Radical Party she was elected to the first parliament of the Second Republic in June 1931, although women still did not have the vote. The franchise was a contentious issue. Liberals argued that women's enfranchisement would increase the power of the clergy whereas socialists and Catholics supported women's suffrage. Campoamor never wavered from her support for women's suffrage, although she faced heckling in Parliament and attacks in private. It has been suggested that her passionate and lucid advocacy of women's suffrage made all the difference to its success, but her own political career suffered. She was distrusted by her colleagues in the Radical Party and was not selected to stand for Parliament in 1933. She left Spain at the outbreak of the Civil War and died in 1972.

placed on their role within the home, reinforced by legislative changes that made divorce illegal and restored male authority within marriage.

How far should we see the results of women's enfranchisement as meagre and how did these compare with the hopes of suffrage campaigners? Suffragists themselves did not necessarily expect that there would be rapid changes in women's position as a result of gaining the vote. In Britain, for example, Millicent

Fawcett wrote that while the vote was the 'very foundation stone of political freedom' and would bring 'enlarged opportunities' and an 'improved status of women', she did not believe that this would happen overnight (Fawcett 1920 in Thane 2001: 258).

There was a great deal to be done even to achieve formal equality between men and women. In many countries in Europe feminists still had to campaign for the franchise. In France the movement extended beyond Paris and in 1929 the most important moderate suffrage group, the Union française pour le suffrage des femmes (French Union for Women's Suffrage) had 100,000 members. Up to 1936 the question was practically never off the political agenda as time and again the Chamber of Deputies expressed their support, only to find any proposals blocked by the Senate. In Britain suffragists had to work hard to ensure that all women were finally included in the franchise, regardless of age, in 1928.

Feminists were active in seeking improvements in women's lives both at the workplace and in the home. They lobbied politicians, took part in government inquiries and, on occasion, organized demonstrations in support of causes as diverse as the right of married women to work, access to birth control information and equality for married women under the law. The feminist movement, as a movement, however, seemed to lack coherence and strength. Membership of general feminist organizations declined and the existence of numerous small, single-issue pressure groups confirmed the impression of fragmentation. Feminists who chose to pursue their goals through mixed-sex political parties, in particular social democratic and communist parties, found it difficult to maintain a distinctive presence. Single-sex organizations, such as suffrage groups, encouraged a sense of solidarity among women and the development of a 'feminist consciousness'. Once they left this environment it was difficult for women to retain their confidence and a sense of autonomy. Moreover, European social democratic parties and other groups on the Left were ambiguous in their attitudes towards women's emancipation. There were extensive debates on the 'woman question' and it was common to find socialists using a rhetoric of sex equality, but it in practice these male-dominated, class-based organizations were reluctant to give priority to gender issues.

Mixed-sex politics

Feminist activists were prepared, however, to fight their corner within the mainstream political parties and saw them as a vehicle for advancing their aims. In Britain over half of the individual members of the Labour Party were women – in 1929 there were 250,000 women in 1,867 sections, while in The Netherlands women's share of the membership of the Social Democratic Workers' Party increased from 20% in 1920 to 33% in 1938. In Austria and Holland just over a third of Social Democratic Party members were women, while in Norway and Sweden the figure was 16% and 14% respectively. In contrast, the proportion of women members was much smaller in France and Belgium, where socialist groups were hostile to gender issues, and in Italy and Spain where fascism was the deciding factor.

Engagement in mixed-sex politics raised a complex set of issues for feminists. What should they do when loyalty to class and party conflicted with their commitment to fight against gender inequalities? What kind of relationship should they have with women involved in feminist organizations? Some issues, such as protective legislation, led to fierce disagreements, whereas campaigns to extend the franchise or to gain access to birth control advice brought women together across party and organizational boundaries. Within their own parties socialist women, in particular, raised feminist concerns, but the extent to which they were willing to press their demands varied between individuals and also between countries.

In Sweden, where the social democrats played an important part in the achievement of political and civil rights for women in the early 1920s, socialist women were successful in ensuring that issues such as birth control, improved housing and the social welfare needs of working-class mothers were placed on the social democratic agenda, and Sweden was one of the first countries to legalize abortion in 1938. This can be contrasted with Norway where women had gained civil rights as early as the nineteenth century in the context of liberal politics. Socialism developed after these gains had been made and there was little cooperation between party members and liberal feminists. This continued into the twentieth century when social democrats remained far less supportive of women's rights than their counterparts in Sweden. Debates over the marriage bar in employment illustrate the differences between them. In Sweden left-wing socialists, social democrats and liberal feminists joined together to wage a strong campaign to ensure that a marriage bar would not be implemented. In Norway, however, the social democrats actually introduced a marriage bar and opposition came from liberal women rather than from socialists (Hagemann 2002).

BOX 5.2

Marriage bar

In the context of mass unemployment in the inter-war years, many governments in Europe, at both a national and at a local level, sought to prevent married women from working in occupations such as the civil service, teaching and nursing.

It was common for feminists within socialist organizations to find themselves adopting complex and varied positions. In Denmark, for example, women had little success in persuading the male leadership to adopt their women-centred agenda. In this case socialist women from middle-class backgrounds joined with feminists in the Danish Women's Society to press for reforms for all women, regardless of class, but this led to conflict with many working-class women in the trade union movement and the Working Women's Association. In Britain the conflicts did not follow class lines in such a clear cut way. Within the Labour Party it was women in official leadership positions who were reluctant to cause disunity by supporting controversial questions such as birth control and they placed emphasis on the importance of women's role within the home as the basis of their citizenship. Other women, in particular, those associated with the socialist group, the Independent Labour Party, fought a sustained campaign in the 1920s to persuade the Labour Party leadership to support birth control and family allowances, to oppose the marriage bar in employment, and to give increased power to the Women's Conference. Their campaigns were generally unsuccessful, but feminists did put welfare on the Labour Party's agenda and helped to bring more women into public life.

Women's organizations

What other spaces could women voters use to make their voices heard? How far can they be viewed as part of the history of feminism? Many women's organizations were formed after the First World War to appeal largely to wives and mothers. They were reluctant to identify themselves with the feminist movement but their activities challenged gender inequalities and, in some instances, conventional gender roles. They all aimed to educate women in the rights and duties of citizenship and provided an avenue through which women could take part in public life. In Denmark, for example, women's organizations, including housewives' associations and women's sections in political parties, ensured that a growing number of women would be drawn into political activity. Reaching a peak in the 1940s and 50s these groups gained representation for their organizations in the official committee system. They might have refused the label feminist, but some of their members had the courage to express support for contraception and abortion. Similarly in England groups such as the Townswomen's Guild and the Women's Institute supported a range of social and economic reforms that would improve women's position, in particular, within the home. By distancing themselves from feminist organizations they were able to attract a large number of housewives and mothers who would otherwise have been put off by negative publicity and they campaigned to remove gender inequalities as well as challenging the imbalance of power between men and women.

It would be a mistake to assume that there was a hard and fast line between feminist and non-feminist organizations. Nonetheless, a failure to identify with feminism meant that there was little sense that women's organizations were part of a collective movement that questioned 'traditional gender' roles and developed a consciousness of solidarity among women. A similar point can be made about the plethora of women's organizations established as part of reconstruction in Germany after the Second World War. Karen Offen argues that their 'failure to re-define a woman's place in society and the family meant that women's "organisations" had replaced the (feminist) women's "movement"' (Offen 2000: 389).

Active citizenship: equality and difference

These ambivalent attitudes draw attention to the difficulties of using the label feminist in any rigid or prescriptive sense and to the diverse ways in which women could view their active citizenship. The impulse to be of service to the broader community could be seen to override the selfish individualism of women's rights and enabled women from different political perspectives to work together for social change, including improvements in women's position. The importance or otherwise of women's self-identification as feminists is then further complicated by the differences between members of those organizations that *were* explicitly feminist. They all had to grapple with the same issues – population questions, motherhood and female employment – that also preoccupied politicians and social reformers in Europe and North America. They could not agree, however, about whether to pursue women's equal rights and personal autonomy or whether to emphasize their needs as mothers and the vital role that they could play in society through their position in the family.

These differing perspectives can be explored through the British context in the 1920s. Many pre-war suffrage organizations continued into the inter-war years – for example, the National Union of Women's Suffrage Societies changed its name to the National Union of Societies for Equal Citizenship in 1919 to reflect its broader agenda. Its declared aim was to achieve equal suffrage and 'all other reforms, economic, legislative and social

---

BOX 5.3

Eleanor Rathbone (1872–1946)

Born in Liverpool, the daughter of an industrialist and Liberal MP, Wlliam Rathbone, Eleanor was the first woman to serve on the Liverpool City Council, 1909–10. She was a member of the executive committee of the National Union of Women's Suffrage Societies but resigned for a short period when the Union formed an alliance with the Labour Party, since she thought this would alienate potential suffrage supporters. She re-joined after the outbreak of war and succeeded Millicent Fawcett as president in 1919 when the Union's name was changed to the National Union of Societies for Equal Citizenship. As a leader of the Family Endowment Society she was one of the most prominent campaigners for family allowances and wrote an influential book on the subject, *The Disinherited Family* (1925). She argued that allowances would enable women to gain economic independence within the family and would help their campaign for equal pay at the workplace. NUSEC accepted family allowances as one of its policies in 1925, but it was a controversial measure which led 'equal rights' feminists to put their energies into other groups. In 1929 Eleanor Rathbone was elected as an independent MP for the Combined British Universities and she took a particular interest in the position of women in India. She shared her life with her friend Elizabeth Macadam and died suddenly of a heart attack in 1946.

---

as are necessary to secure a real equality of liberties, status and opportunities between men and women' (Kent 1993: 115). The meaning of equality, however, was hotly contested. The president of NUSEC, Eleanor Rathbone, argued that women could never achieve equality unless their special needs as mothers were addressed, in particular their economic dependence on men, and she advocated a range of social reforms, including family allowances, to improve women's status within the home. This position has been labelled as 'new feminism'.

Others, who have been described as 'old' feminists, continued to focus on equal rights. Differences between the two groups should not be exaggerated, since in practice most feminists sought to extend equal rights and also supported welfare measures that would improve the lives of working-class mothers. Nonetheless, there were differences in the assumptions underlying those reforms. 'New' feminists referred to maternity as 'the most important of women's occupations', while 'equality' feminists were concerned that a focus on motherhood would make it difficult for women to escape from traditional roles and preferred to emphasize the 'common humanity of men and women' (Smith 1990: 47–65).

Similar debates took place elsewhere. Protective legislation for women workers was particularly contentious, causing disagreements between feminists from all shades of the political spectrum. In the United States, for example, Alice Paul proposed an Equal Rights Amendment to the constitution in 1923 which read that 'men and women shall have equal rights throughout the United States'. She argued that this would remove legal barriers to women's advancement in the public sphere and that this would then be followed by changes in the family and the relationship between the sexes. Her views were bitterly opposed by other groups, such as the League of Women Voters, who thought priority should be given to the welfare needs of working-class mothers and to women's role within the family. They pushed for more rather than less protective legislation to shorten hours of work and to regulate the conditions of women's employment. In Britain protective legislation was one of the issues that made it difficult for feminists within the labour movement to work with those who were outside. It also created a split within the feminist organization, NUSEC, when those opposed to protective legislation established the Open Door Council in 1927. These conflicts spilled over into feminist international organizations as laws regulating women's labour became an international issue. Disagreements came to a head at the 1926 IWSA Congress when Alice Paul's National Woman Party applied to affiliate. Subsequently new organizations, such as the Open Door International, were formed to lead the fight against protective legislation.

Welfare feminism

Protective legislation was so contentious because it raised the difficult question of whether women, because of their marginal position in employment, should be treated differently from men. Disagreements over other social welfare proposals tended to focus on the form that they took rather than on whether they should be introduced in the first place. The state provision of economic assistance to families was a common demand from feminists in countries as diverse as Britain, Germany and Scandinavia. They added their voices to a more general demand that family allowances should be introduced but disagreed on how such allowances should be financed and what they hoped to achieve by their introduction. In Norway, for instance, liberal and conservative women argued that regular wages should support only one individual with allowances given for the number of children in a household, whereas socialist women wanted a 'mother's wage' financed through the tax system. They saw this as a means to free women from work outside the home, enabling them to devote more time to their children. Liberal feminists, however, saw child allowances as a way that mothers could pay for child care and therefore continue with paid employment. In Britain, Eleanor Rathbone thought that family allowances would bring economic independence for mothers within the home and would strengthen the case for equal pay at the workplace. She accepted that some married women might wish to seek paid employment, but her emphasis was on the importance of women from all social classes placing greater value on motherhood.

The feminist dimension of proposals for family allowances could easily get lost within arguments that emphasized the relationship between welfare policies, child poverty and population growth. In contrast, campaigns for reproductive rights appeared to have a greater potential for challenging traditional structures since they raised issues about women's autonomy and personal freedom. The 1920s provided a new context for advocates of birth control. The First World War had brought a change in attitudes to sex and morality, while for a brief period debates on the 'woman question' in Bolshevik Russia included an emphasis on sexual freedoms. Alexandra Kollontai's writings expressed the view that men and women could be 'lovers and comrades outside structures that formalised relationships characterised by domination and subordination' (Offen 2000: 268) and legislation was introduced on birth control and abortion. However, the association of birth control with 'free love', coupled with the opposition of governments anxious to promote more births, meant that feminist groups were cautious in their approach to the question. In many countries it was socialist women who took the lead in demanding the provision of free contraceptive advice. Nonetheless, in both cases feminists downplayed the importance of women achieving sexual autonomy and emphasized the health and welfare aspects of birth control, with socialist women raising the class dimensions of the issue. Indeed, many feminists were still more concerned with controlling male sexuality than with seeking sexual freedom for women.

Welfare feminism did have a radical potential, since it raised fundamental questions about the role of women in the family and could draw working-class women into a feminist constituency. However, this potential was rarely realized. Few analytical connections were made between the family and other social structures, while the critical edge of 'new feminists' was blunted by using women's needs as mothers, rather than their rights as women, as a basis on which to demand reform. As Susan Kingsley Kent, a leading historian of the war and post-war period notes, 'when 'new feminists made demands based upon women's traditional, special needs and special functions, when they ceased to challenge the dominant discourses on sexuality, their ideology often became confused with anti-feminists' (Kent 1993: 118). Eleanor Rathbone's arguments for family allowances are a case in point. Although she believed that allowances would provide economic independence for married women, she also suggested that they would alleviate child poverty and improve the quality of the population – views that were indistinguishable from reformers who did not have a feminist perspective.

In Scandinavian countries however, women played an important part in shaping the social welfare measures that were introduced by social democratic parties in the 1930s. In Sweden these included job protection for pregnant women, the legalization of contraception and maternity benefits that were paid to mothers, while in Sweden and Denmark abortion based on a restricted set of criteria was also made legal. It was the Swedish feminist Alva Myrdal who made some of the most radical suggestions for enabling women to combine motherhood and paid employment. She called for child care facilities, a range of social services, social support for domestic labour and a change in the division of labour within the home so that women would no longer have a 'double burden'. She framed her proposals in terms of Sweden's national interest, since mothers would not only have economic independence but would live in stable heterosexual partnerships and bear healthy children. Her views were too radical for the inter-war years, but many of her ideas were implemented in Sweden in the 1960s.

How far were women's campaigns responsible for the welfare reforms that were introduced? It was far easier for feminists to make gains when their aims coincided with those of the parties in power. In the United States, where women had a high public visibility in the 1930s, Eleanor Roosevelt was able to take advantage of a favourable political climate to gain humanitarian reforms. In Denmark, Sweden and Norway social democratic parties introduced social welfare reforms that benefited women, but they were financed through direct taxation and were intended to redistribute resources as well as to improve the lives of the poor. Feminists within these parties had to battle much harder to gain support for the legalization of birth control information and abortion. In Britain too it was not until 1930 that the Labour government finally conceded that local authority clinics could give birth control information to married women. Family allowances were resisted in the inter-war years and faced considerable opposition from the trade union movement. When they were finally introduced after the Second World War the intention was to reduce wage inflation rather than to ensure the economic independence of married women.

Feminism and peace

The key issue was not whether social welfare measures were introduced, but whether they shifted the power relationship between men and women and challenged gender divisions. Many feminists were clear that an emphasis on social welfare did neither of these things and that feminist goals could easily be subsumed within a broader movement. Similar issues were raised by the involvement of women in international issues, in particular the movement for peace. The Women's International League for Peace and Freedom was the main rallying point for those feminists who sought to focus their efforts on peace, democracy and freedom, although the International Women Suffrage Alliance, later the International Alliance of Women, also worked for peace as one of its aims. There had been a long-standing connection between feminism and peace, stretching back to the nineteenth century. During the First World War it was difficult for all but a minority of women to make a stand for peace, but in the aftermath of that conflict women joined in vigorously to add their voices to those who insisted that such a war should never happen again. Peace raised in an acute form the different positions of men and women. War was seen to be an outcome of male values of aggression and ambition compared with female values of care for others, sacrifice and love.

Feminists who took a more radical perspective also drew attention to the violence that men perpetrated against women in time of war. It was assumed that men actually enjoyed fighting and conquest. Carrie Chapman Catt expressed the views of many in the days before women were enfranchised that 'all wars are men's wars. Peace has been made by women, but wars never' (quoted in Rupp 1997: 84). Suffragists, in particular, argued that once women were able to influence foreign policy then they would be a force for peace, progress and civilization against war and barbarism. It became more common for peace campaigners during and after the First World War to argue that mothers in particular had a horror of war since they created the life that wars destroyed. Even those who were not mothers could empathize with this argument since all women were viewed as having a caring and nurturing role, both in the family and in the wider community. It was assumed therefore that a hatred of war had the potential to unite women across national boundaries in a common action.

Nonetheless, peace was another issue that that strained the common bonds between women. The 'equal rights' activist Nina Boyle, for example, argued that feminists were diverted away from a focus on women's legal and material subordination to men if they took up causes such as pacifism and social reform. Others disagreed and positively welcomed the view that feminism should encompass a broad agenda. Indeed, Carrie Chapman Catt claimed that 'I have personally moved on and become a humanist since the vote came to me', but 'I have not ceased to be a feminist nor to be less sympathetic with protests against women's wrongs' (Offen 2000: 375, 371). Despite such protestations, if women's emancipation became tied up with the defence of democracy and freedom for both sexes then gender inequalities and issues around male power over women could easily slip from view. This is yet another reason why inter-war feminism in Europe and North America could appear to be more fragmented and diffuse than in the pre-war years.

In a hostile political and economic climate feminists did continue to campaign for reforms and to challenge gender inequalities. They worked through a wide range of groups, including single-sex feminist organizations, women's groups, political parties and peace organizations. This meant that they were less visible as part of a vibrant movement, but it did give them a platform from which to raise issues of concern to women. Feminists debated what it meant to be a citizen and tried to extend the gains already made in equal rights. Many also focused on the needs of the working-class woman and campaigned for social welfare reforms, ranging from improved health care facilities to reproductive rights. For some feminists women's role as wives and mothers provided the basis from which they could play a part as active citizens, although this was a controversial point of view. In several countries women's groups, representing housewives, were drawn into the official committee system and were called on to give advice to governments. It was far more difficult for women to assert their rights to active citizenship as waged workers, in particular in the context of economic depression and the rise of conservative and fascist governments. It was not until the 1960s and 70s that feminists were able to make a sustained challenge to women's identification with the home and to put to the test con-temporary assumptions about appropriate male and female roles.

Further reading

For a clear discussion of the inter-war context, see Marlene Legates, *In Their Time: A History of Feminism in Western Society*, London: Routledge, 2001, Ch. 9; and Gisela Bock, *Women in European History*, Oxford: Blackwell, 2001. For developments in particular countries, see Karen Offen, *European Feminisms, 1700–1950*, Stanford, CA: Stanford University Press, 2000; and Gabriele Griffin and Rosi Braidotti (eds) *Thinking Differently: A Reader in European Women's Studies*, London: Zed Books, 2002. Johanna Alberti, *Beyond Suffrage: Feminists in War and Peace, 1914–28*, Houndmills: Macmillan, 1989 explores the biographies of 14 British activists and argues that there were continuities between the ideas and aspirations of feminists before, during and after the First World War. Susan Kingsley Kent, however, claims that the war altered the language of gender relations and that this changed the terms available for inter-war feminists to express their ideas: *Making Peace: The Reconstruction of Gender in Inter-War Britain*, Princeton, NJ: Princeton University Press, 1993.

Statistics of women's participation in representative assemblies can be found in Melanie Nolan and Caroline Daley, 'International Feminist Perspectives on Suffrage: An Introduction', in Caroline Daley and Melanie Nolan (eds) *Suffrage and Beyond: International Feminist Perspectives*, Auckland: Auckland University Press, 1994. The difficulties feminists encountered in societies where the Catholic Church and conservative governments emphasized traditional family structures and roles are explored in: Margaret

Ward, *Unmanageable Revolutionaries. Women and Irish Nationalism*, London: Pluto Press, 1983; Margaret Ward, ' "Suffrage First – Above All Else!" An Account of the Irish Suffrage Movement', in Alibhe Smyth (ed.) *Irish Women's Studies Reader*, Dublin: Attic Press, 1993; and Judith Keene, ' "Into the Clean Air of the Plaza": Spanish Women Achieve the Vote in 1931', in Victoria Loree Enders and Pamela Beth Radcliff (eds) *Constructing Spanish Womanhood: Female Identity in Modern Spain*, Albany, NY: State University of New York Press, 1999.

The ways in which social democratic parties in a variety of European countries engaged with feminism and 'women's emancipation' are explored in a series of essays in Helmut Gruber and Pamela Graves (eds) *Women and Socialism, Socialism and Women. Europe Between the Two World Wars*, Oxford: Berghahn, 1998. In Britain, Alberti, *Beyond Suffrage* (above), suggests that the involvement of women in the labour movement strained feminist solidarity in the 1920s while Harold L. Smith argues that the leaders of the Labour Party were actively hostile to feminists outside the movement and ensured that class interests would be paramount within the Party: Harold L. Smith, 'Sex Vs Class: British Feminists and the Labour Movement, 1919–29', *Historian*, 47, 1984, pp. 19–37. Pat Thane, on the other hand, suggests that Labour women wanted women to have real choices in their lives, put welfare on the Labour Party's agenda, helped to improve local welfare services, and also brought more women into public life: 'Women in the British Labour Party and the Construction of State Welfare', in Seth Koven and Sonya Michel (eds) *Mothers of a New World: Maternalist Politics and the Origins of the Welfare States*, London: Routledge, 1993. For a comparison of social democratic parties in Norway and Sweden, see Gro

Hagemann, 'Citizenship and Social Order: Gender Politics in Twentieth Century Norway and Sweden', *Women's History Review*, 11, 3, 2002.

A stimulating re-assessment of what suffrage campaigners in Britain hoped to achieve once the vote was won is put forward by Pat Thane, 'What Difference Did the Vote Make', in Amanda Vickery (ed.) *Women, Privilege and Power. British Politics 1750 to the Present*, Stanford, CA: Stanford University Press, 2001. Cheryl Law, *Suffrage and Power: The Women's Movement 1918–1928*, London: I.B. Tauris, 1998 examines the neglected campaign to extend the franchise to all adult women in Britain in the 1920s. The various contributors to Harold L. Smith (ed.) *British Feminism in the Twentieth Century*, Aldershot: Edward Elgar, 1990 urge caution in drawing a rigid distinction between 'old' and 'new' feminists and also between concepts of equality and difference in the inter-war years. Caitriona Beaumont extends the discussion about definitions of feminism by arguing that a wider range of women's organizations should be included: 'Citizens not Feminists: The Boundary Negotiated between Citizenship and Feminism by Mainstream Women's Organisations in England, 1928–39', *Women's History Review*, 9, 2, 2000. The debates in European inter-war feminism about social welfare, protective legislation and reproductive rights are explored in Offen *European Feminisms* (above); Gruber and Graves, *Socialism and Women* (above); Smith, *British Feminism* (above). All of these give an extensive guide to further reading. For the conflict in the United States over protective legislation, see Barbara Ryan, *Feminism and the Women's Movement. Dynamics of Change in Social Movement, Ideology and Activism*, London: Routledge, 1992. Recent texts that discuss the interrelationship between inter-war feminism and peace movements include: Leila Rupp, *Worlds of Women: The Making of an International Women's Movement*, Princeton, NJ: Princeton University Press, 1997; and Christine Bolt, *Sisterhood Questioned: Race, Class and Internationalism in the American and British Women's Movements c. 1800s–1970*, London: Routledge, 2004.

CHAPTER 6

The 'personal is political': women's liberation and 'second wave feminism'

IN 1968 WOMEN IN ATLANTIC CITY DECIDED to stage a protest against the Miss America beauty contest. They invited women to throw their bras and girdles, symbols of the pressures on women to conform to unrealistic standards of beauty, into a 'freedom trash bucket'. This was the start of a new and explosive period in feminist history. A series of provocative direct actions followed and soon attracted the attention of the world's media. The women's liberation movement, as it was popularly called, swept through North America and western Europe. For almost a decade this vibrant political force was rarely out of the headlines. It was the first time in two generations that women 'unapologetically declared their feminism' (Legates 2001: 327) and the movement soon became known as 'second wave feminism'.

Origins of 'second wave feminism'

What led women to take such flamboyant and public actions?
Why was 1968 a crucial turning point? Some of the answers must
be looked for as far back as the Second World War. Women's
expectations were raised as a result of their extensive participation in the war effort – as workers, members of the armed forces
and as activists in the resistance. In France (1944) and Italy
(1945) women finally gained the right to vote, while in the atmos-
phere of liberation after the war feminists demanded full civil
rights for women. In France, for instance, pre-war suffragists,
resistance workers and Catholic women joined together to
ensure that the new Constitution in France would include a
clause on sexual equality in all areas of life, including family law,
as well as a guarantee that mothers and their children would
receive protection.

Formal equality, however, did not automatically mean that
women experienced a fundamental change in their social and
economic position. A fear of social instability after the upheavals
of war led governments to emphasize the importance of
'traditional' gender roles. Social welfare policies, for instance,
including family allowances and social security payments, were
based on the assumption that there was a male breadwinner. The
image of the contented wife and mother, giving all her attention
to housework, children and the care of her husband was widespread in popular magazines and advertisements. It is hardly
surprising, therefore, that the 1950s has been described as the
'decade of the housewife'. As the political landscape became more
conservative it proved increasingly difficult for feminists to find
a space to put forward alternative views. During the Cold War,

in countries dominated by the Soviet Union only Communist Party sponsored organizations were allowed to thrive, while governments in the West were suspicious of any movements that appeared 'radical' or subversive. In this climate 'traditional' family roles were seen as crucial for social stability. In Spain, for example, under the authoritarian regime of General Franco, women were expected to devote themselves to the family and had few personal or social rights. In Catholic countries such as Italy and Ireland women were subordinate to male relatives within the family and in the 1950s and 60s suffered from discriminatory legislation relating to divorce, adultery and abortion.

BOX 6.1

Simone De Beauvoir, 1908–86

Born in Paris, De Beauvoir studied at the Sorbonne where, in 1929, she met Jean-Paul Sartre. Through their lifelong friendship she contributed to the development of existentialist philosophy and she became well known as a novelist, political theorist, essayist and biographer. *Le Deuxième Sexe (The Second Sex)*, published first in French in 1949, provided a detailed analysis of women's oppression. Her existentialist views were evident when she argued that existence precedes essence – hence, one was not born but became a woman. De Beauvoir argued that the assumption that men represented the norm, and that women, throughout history, had been seen to deviate from this, limited women's sense of themselves and their possibilities since they were always viewed as 'the other'. This, coupled with her assertion that women were as capable of choice as men, provided feminists with a new way of understanding the social position of women and helps to explain the impact of her book.

And yet women did not remain silent. They continued to organize together to demand improvements in their employment and family lives, working through trade unions and political parties as well as their own single-sex organizations. Debates about gender roles were fuelled by key pieces of writing. Simone De Beauvoir's *The Second Sex* (1949) was a particularly influential text.

De Beauvoir argued that women did not have a clear identity of their own since they were always viewed as 'the other' in relation to men. She emphasized that the roles and characteristics assigned to women were socially constructed. In a famous passage she concluded that 'one is not born, but rather becomes, a woman', since a woman's 'destiny is imposed upon her by her teachers and her society' (De Beauvoir 1953: 315). De Beauvoir did not see herself as writing in a feminist tradition but tried to understand women's subordination in the context of her broader interest in existentialist philosophy. Nonetheless, her work was to become a key foundation text for 'second wave feminism'.

The image of the perfect wife and mother was increasingly at odds with the realities of women's lives in the late 1950s and 1960s. As young women took advantage of the opportunities offered by an expansion in higher education they were less content than their mothers to accept a future bounded by domesticity. At the same time married women began to enter the labour force in larger numbers. They were clustered in part-time and low-paid work that prompted extensive public debates and government inquiries into gender inequalities at the workplace, many of which resulted in legislation. In Norway, for example, the principle of equal pay was adopted in 1958 and a new taxation system for married couples was introduced, weakening the male breadwinner system. In Canada a number of women's organizations came together in 1966 to put pressure on the government to appoint a Royal Commission on women, while in France public discussion on women's work outside the home contributed to a reform of the law on marriage in 1965.

The 1960s also saw the publication of another key text, Betty Friedan's *The Feminine Mystique* (1963). This seemed to encapsulate the frustrations of white, middle-class housewives in suburban America who, when interviewed, suggested that their lives had not been fulfilled. Friedan labelled this as 'the problem with no name'. She explored how women had come to believe that they should be good wives and mothers and therefore blamed themselves if they failed to be contented with their roles. Friedan's solution for this problem was to encourage women to take up paid employment, although she perhaps underestimated the difficulties of combining paid work and child care. She also gave too much emphasis to the bored housewife and said little about those women who were active outside the home in voluntary social or political work. Nonetheless, she was important in drawing attention to 'sex role conditioning' and to the fact that nurture, rather than nature, had assigned women to domestic roles. She stimulated debates about the position of women, in particular, on women's experiences within the family – a question that was to be central for 'second wave feminism'.

Protest in the 1960s

It was the black civil rights movement, however, that provided the main impetus for women to organize together and to challenge contemporary gender roles. By taking part in the movement they established networks, learned new tactics and also began to raise questions about their own lack of rights. In 1966 Betty Friedan, along with labour and civil rights activists, established the National Organization of Women (NOW) to 'bring women into full participation in the mainstream of American society now' (Legates 2001: 348).

NOW can be located in many respects in a long-standing liberal tradition that emphasized the importance of men and

---

BOX 6.2

National Organization for Women

The National Organization for Women (NOW) was founded by Betty Friedan and other feminist leaders in 1966. At its first conference in Washington NOW declared that its aims were to bring women into full participation in the mainstream of American society so that they could reach their full potential as human beings. It sought to use the law to gain equality of opportunity in employment and education and to achieve equal civil and political rights and responsibilities for women. It spearheaded women's growing involvement in political campaigns and called for women to speak out for their own rights in partnership with men. NOW has continued to help women and to act as a pressure group up to the present day. It has mobilized numerous mass demonstrations – for example, in 1978 100,000 people marched in favour of an Equal Rights Amendment to the Constitution and there have been several Marches for Women's Lives for reproductive rights, culminating in a demonstration of 1.15 million people in 2004. NOW currently has 500,000 members and its priorities include economic equality, an equal rights amendment to the Constitution, abortion rights and reproductive freedom, ending violence against women and opposition to racism and bigotry against lesbians and gays.

women working together to achieve change through legislation. Nonetheless, by 1967 its members had begun to take more radical direct action, picketing government offices to ensure that laws were complied with. Just as pressure began to mount for more attention to be paid to gender inequalities, student unrest and demonstrations against the Vietnam War in 1968 were to transform the political landscape.

Across Europe and North America students took to the streets to protest against the Vietnam War, to call for reforms in education and to demand civil freedoms. Inspired by revolutionary struggles elsewhere in the world they criticized the capitalist system and, in Paris, were joined by workers from a range of industries who went on strike. Grass-roots action and street demonstrations, in which there were violent confrontations with the police, characterized the movement. Women joined into these activities with enthusiasm but too often ended up as caterers and minute takers rather than as speakers and decision takers. Their frustration at being marginalized was increased by the fact that this was 'flagrantly contradicting the anti hierarchical and participatory ideals of the 1968 movements' (Eley 2002: 366). When they demanded a greater role women found that men, who claimed to be their comrades, did not take them seriously and were 'sexist' in their attitudes. This prompted women to draw attention to the specific problems that they faced as women and to question the priorities and concerns of a male-defined left politics.

It is hardly surprising, therefore, that women began to meet together in autonomous single-sex groups to discuss issues that concerned them and to raise their own demands. Inspired by the demonstration against the Miss World contest in Atlantic City women in America and elsewhere took direct action to draw attention to their grievances. In Germany women members of the Socialist German Student Federation met to discuss their specific problems, in particular child care, and argued that the family, as well as the workplace or the university, should become a site of political activity. When they met with derision from men at a subsequent conference one woman pelted her critics with tomatoes. French women also rejected the 'sexism' of the Left. They formed numerous women-only groups, including the MLF (Mouvement de libération des femmes). Some of these groups wanted to work anonymously underground whereas others, following the provocative style of May '68, carried out spectacular public actions, using 'transgression, insolence and caustic humour to win the media's attention' (Picq 2002: 316). The most famous example was when one woman laid a wreath of flowers under the Arc de Triomphe for the wife of the unknown soldier. In 1971 over 300 French women signed a newspaper article, known as the 'Whore's Manifesto', declaring that they had had an illegal abortion and this was followed by a similar public declaration in West Germany.

In Britain the women's liberation movement gained an impetus from the campaign of women factory workers for equal pay as well as from disillusion with the attitudes of men in the anti-Vietnam War protests. The first Women's Liberation Conference, attended by over 600 women, was held at Ruskin College early in 1970. A National Women's Coordinating Committee was formed to demand equal pay, equal education and employment opportunities, free contraception and abortion on demand and 24-hour nurseries. Disruptive actions were also common. In 1969 the Tufnell Park women's liberation group leafleted the Ideal

Home Exhibition and a year later there was a protest against the televised Miss World Competition at the Albert Hall in which protesters threw smoke bombs and bags of flour.

The women's liberation movement was not just confined to Europe and North America. Japanese feminists, for example, highlighted inequalities in family law and the problems of working women. They organized demonstrations and sit-ins and campaigned to have a 'sexist' television commercial for instant noodles removed. In Scandinavia, however, where legal equalities in marriage and the right to abortion had already been achieved, and where social welfare legislation enabled women to combine work and family, a women's liberation movement was far less evident.

Characteristics of the women's liberation movement

Feminists did not always agree on the best way to organize and on the demands that they wanted to make. In France, Germany, Italy and the United States there was an emphasis on women working autonomously in single-sex groups. In the United States, in particular, feminists tried to develop a separate women's culture and placed emphasis on sex oppression. In Britain, however, class politics exerted more influence and many feminists sought to maintain links with the trade union and labour movement. And yet with their slogan 'sisterhood is powerful' women sought to transcend their differences and had a sense that they were part of an international movement with shared characteristics.

Autonomous women's groups were at the heart of the women's liberation movement. Formed at a grass-roots level and outside of existing political parties, they deliberately rejected hierarchies and national leaders. At meetings individual women were encouraged to speak about their own experiences. Consciousness raising, as it was termed, was intended to help women to develop an awareness of their position and to take control over their own lives and aspirations. As they talked about the frustrations that they experienced in their private lives women came to realize that their difficulties were not just individual ones but arose from social conditions that were shared by others. This self-knowledge was then a springboard for taking collective actions to achieve change. These could be spontaneous, unplanned actions including 'sudden outbreaks of anger, gatherings with singing, dancing through the streets, impromptu speeches and exuberant expressions of solidarity' (Kaplan 1992: 19). They could also be well-organized events such as sit-ins, marches and demonstrations. For example, in 1977–8 women marched through the streets in Britain, West Germany and Italy in 'Reclaim the Night' actions to assert their right to be in public spaces in safety after dark.

The 'personal is political' was one of the most famous slogans of the movement. Women were expected to conform to particular ideals of femininity and this affected the ways in which they thought about themselves as well as simply being imposed from outside. Feminists consistently drew attention to the way in which consumerism and advertising used women's sexuality to sell goods and conditioned them into believing that only a particular kind of beauty had value. This encouraged women to spend a great deal of money on the latest fashions and beauty products. It also fed into anxieties about ageing and the 'ideal body shape' that could lead to cosmetic surgery and eating disorders so graphically portrayed in Susie Orbach's *Fat is a Feminist Issue* (1981). Areas once thought as private, including anxieties about the body, sexuality and relationships between men and women were all viewed as political issues within 'second wave feminism'. The pleasures of sex and women's erotic desires were emphasized as well as women's right to define their own sexuality and the demand that there should be an end to discrimination against lesbians. Consciousness raising played a central role in ensuring that the personal would become political and women were encouraged to 'reassess their personal and emotional lives, their relation to their families, their lovers and their work' and to 'negotiate an autonomous identity beyond those associated with family duties' (Whelehan 1995: 13).

The family was viewed as a key site of women's oppression. Alongside more conventional demands for equal pay and an end to sex discrimination at work feminists called for paid housework, child care facilities, and contraceptive advice. Reproductive rights, including free contraception and abortion on demand, were central issues for the women's liberation movement. Campaigns to legalize abortion, and to ensure that women had the right to choose whether to have an abortion, took place in most countries in Europe and North America in the early 1970s. It was the one issue that managed to bring women from different generations, social groups and political backgrounds together at a national level to work for a reform of common concern. For the most part, these campaigns were successful in legalizing abortion, but the legislation often fell short of the demand for a woman's right to choose.

Feminists communicated their ideas through an array of newspapers, newsletters and journals and also through women's presses, such as Virago in Britain and Arlen House in Ireland. Education also provided an important space for feminists to challenge conventional wisdoms about gender roles and contemporary definitions of femininity. As more women entered higher education, they highlighted the fact that women were invisible in academic disciplines that had been defined by men. They demanded women's studies courses to provide information about women's lives and to raise new questions about how knowledge had been constructed. This in turn affected the nature of the academic disciplines themselves. Women's studies courses also had a role to play in the political struggle for women's liberation. An important part of the academic project, for example, was to re-discover women's political activism in the past – pioneering texts included Sheila Rowbotham's *Hidden From History* and Gerda Lerner's *The Majority Finds Its Past*. As feminists found out more about the varied activities in which women had been involved in the past so they were able to question the view that women's roles were natural and could not be changed.

Key texts of 'second wave feminism'

A number of key texts helped to shape the ideas and characteristics of the early years of the women's liberation movement. 'Liberal feminists' still focused on individual rights and equal opportunities and argued that legal and social policy changes would help women to achieve these. More characteristic of 'second wave feminism', however, was the 'radical feminist' attempt to find new ways of theorizing women's relationship to men. They looked in particular at 'men's social control of women through various mechanisms of patriarchy . . . especially violence, heterosexuality and reproduction, where men as a group are seen as responsible for maintaining women's oppression' (Maynard 1998: 253). Kate Millett's influential book *Sexual Politics* (1969) argued that patriarchy, or male power over women, underpinned all social forms including the family, religion and the workplace. The fact that patriarchy was all pervasive and also operated at the level of ideas meant that it had the power to shape how women thought as well as how they lived their lives. By suggesting that personal lives were affected by the state and by patriarchy, Millett opened the way for feminists to challenge the division between the public and the private that was central to liberal political thought. Millett's scathing attack on male authors for glorifying sexual brutality against women in literature brought her considerable notoriety and criticism for being anti-male.

Germaine Greer, an Australian academic living in England, also became the centre of controversy for her book *The Female Eunuch* (1971). This was a provocative text that led to criticism from both within and outside the women's liberation movement. Greer produced a polemic about the ways in which women had been conditioned to accept a sense of inferiority to men and argued for sexual liberation outside the monogamous family. She made a spirited attack on the constraints women faced in their lives but was criticized by many feminists for blaming women themselves for failing to grasp the opportunities that were offered. She complained that women were 'frigid' and argued that 'the cage door has been opened but the canary has refused to fly out' (p. 14). With her tall, striking figure and her views on the enjoyment of heterosexual sex, Greer was described by *Life* magazine as the 'saucy feminist that even men like' and it is not surprising that she stood outside the mainstream.

Within Britain, in particular, women who had taken part in left politics attempted to bring together a Marxist and a feminist approach in which the economic roots of women's exploitation within capitalism could be linked with more personal forms of oppression. In her influential text *Woman's Estate* (1974), for example, Juliet Mitchell revised standard Marxist accounts by analysing the position of women not just in terms of relations of production or of private property but also by looking at sexual differences through the insights offered by psychoanalytic theory.

The lively debate among feminists about the root causes of women's oppression and about the nature and importance of patriarchy provides just one example of the vibrancy of the women's movement in the early 1970s. This was a time of exceptional activity as women mobilized across several countries. Contemporaries self-consciously described themselves as feminists and felt that they were taking part in a new phenomenon. In France, for example, feminists proclaimed 'women's liberation, year zero' in 1970 to demonstrate that they had different goals and a different way of thinking than the liberal feminists who had preceded them. Clearly there were many similarities with feminist campaigners of previous generations. 'Second wave feminists' pursued a variety of equal rights campaigns alongside other demands and some of the direct actions and use of spectacle evoked the militancy of the British suffragettes. Nonetheless, there were differences. In Britain, young middle-class women did support campaigns for equal rights at work, but their passionate, personal concerns were about 'images in advertising, child care, the response of left-wing men to women's liberation' (Rowbotham 1989: 166). The language used was significant; emancipation implied freedom from constraints and the achievement of social policies to enable women to fulfil their potential. Liberation, on the other hand, implied a greater sense of personal empowerment and choice, adventure and sexual power free from prevailing ideas of what it meant to be a woman. More women were now prepared to take part in exuberant actions. They organized from the grass roots, were suspicious of charismatic leaders and put 'personal' issues such as the control of their own bodies and sexual freedoms at the forefront of their politics. The style of the movement was subversive. 'It meant taking the culture's trappings and symbols, its most cherished beliefs and disordering them, playing with them, turning their meanings around in acts of public transgression. It was a calculated acting out, a purposeful disobedience, a misbehaving in public' (Eley 2002: 372).

Decade of women, 1976–85

The mobilization of so many women, and the publicity given to the inequalities and discrimination faced by women throughout the world, contributed to the United Nations designating 1975 as International Women's Year and then instituting the Decade for Women, 1976–85. The UN called on governments to improve health, employment and educational levels of women under the banner of equality, development and peace. This provided a stimulus for women across the world to set up women's groups and to make their own demands. In Japan, for example, the International Women's Year Action Group was able to exert pressure for change on the government at home as well as raising issues in the International Women's Decade conferences held at Copenhagen, Mexico and Nairobi. In Brazil the military government allowed International Women's Day to be celebrated in 1975 since women were not seen as 'political'. This gave a stimulus to feminist demands. At first these focused on women's work and production, but at the 1978 International Women's Day the politics of the private sphere, the family and reproductive rights were highlighted.

Women in Third World countries had their own independent goals and strategies. In India, for example, a countrywide movement of women emerged on a mass scale in 1979–80 when the Supreme Court acquitted a policeman accused of raping a young woman who was in custody. Women took part in mass demonstrations and established organizations such as the Joint Women's Programme (1981) and the India Democratic Women's Association (1981) to fight all forms of violence against women, including the practice of sati and dowry deaths. Some groups were locally based and autonomous, drawing their active supporters from young, educated urban feminists who had worked with women in rural areas, slums and trade unions. Others were affiliated with various political parties and sought to make gains for women through existing political channels as well as through direct actions.

'Second wave' feminism in Latin America

Women also mobilized on a large scale in Latin America in the 1970s and 80s. Their political strategies, however, were complex and their movements arose within a very different context to that found in Europe and North America. The repression of political parties and trade unions opened up a space for women to play a key role in campaigns to achieve democracy and they were then inspired to raise their own demands as a sex. Women were involved in three different types of action. In response to the economic difficulties facing their families working-class women joined together at a grass-roots level to ensure access to basic services that were being neglected by their governments. Women also organized as mothers to demand information about missing relatives, in particular their children and grandchildren, and raised human-rights questions. The most famous of the groups were the *Madres de la Plaza de Mayo* in Argentina. In both of these cases women used their traditional role as wives and mothers as a justification for their political activism and did not initially draw attention to gender-specific issues.

Alongside these groups, however, educated middle-class women, many of whom were active in left opposition parties, began to raise questions about sex discrimination in the context of the larger class struggle and also established separate women's groups. For example, when the Echeverría regime in Mexico allowed new opposition parties to form from 1970–6 young professional women and students formed feminist organizations. They emphasized the need for consciousness raising and held workshops and demonstrations, often criticizing consumerism and its exploitation of women. In raising the question of what democratization would mean for women, feminists in Latin American countries linked the authoritarianism of the state with authoritarianism in society, in particular the family, and argued that sex oppression lay at the root of most social structures. Their demands mirrored those of their counterparts in the West, ranging from economic and equal rights issues to questions of reproduction and male violence.

The dynamism and variety of the feminist movement in Latin America can be seen in the debates at the biennial *encuentros* (conventions) held in the area during the 1980s. These provided a stimulus to movements in particular countries and also revealed the changing concerns of feminists over time as attendance expanded to include women from Central and South America and from the Caribbean. In Bogotá in 1981 the key debates were over autonomy from mainstream politics and whether feminist objectives could be separated from the class struggle. In Lima in 1983 the theme was patriarchy. The inclusion of members of the popular, grass-roots women's movements expanded the parameters of the debate about autonomy since for some it 'opened up the possibility that women could define and act on their own interests' (Jaquette 1994: 5). In São Paulo, Brazil, in 1985 race and sexual preference were part of the agenda in an explicit way for the first time, although class remained a central issue.

Sex, race and class

For Third World feminists it was impossible to disentangle sex from race and class oppression. In South Africa, for example, black women took part in the struggle against apartheid and also had to cope with the absence of male members of the family. Their priorities were to ensure the economic and physical survival of their families. This entailed working long hours for low pay as well as providing many of the primary health-care services. Thus, the dichotomy between public and private spheres, and between masculine and feminine domains, was less marked in African societies than in many other countries. African feminism therefore stressed 'human totality, parallel autonomy, co-operation, self reliance, adaptation, survival and liberation' (Steady 1996: 18). Women's role in ensuring family survival led to grass-roots organizing at community level and then to involvement in national and international politics.

In practice there were many overlaps between women's groups that had practical goals, such as the protection of families, and those that highlighted gender inequalities. Women in opposition movements in Latin America used their 'traditional' social role as mothers as a source of strength and were able to create a new feminist practice as they politicized everyday life. In Brazil, for example, housewives who engaged in community politics also began to discuss family, love and childbearing and increasingly focused on women's subordination. This in turn had an influence on the agenda of the middle-class feminist movement. By the late 1970s the feminist movement had reached women from all social classes, had expanded the definition of feminist struggle and had formed new groups, including those based on the needs and specific agendas of Afro-Brazilians and lesbians (Alvarez 1994: 25).

Divisions in 'second wave' feminism

A sense of 'sisterhood', so integral to the women's liberation movement in Europe and North America, was difficult to sustain as differences based on class, race and sexual orientation increasingly came to the surface. 'Second wave feminism' was dominated by white, educated, middle-class, heterosexual women and their concerns. The methods used, in particular, consciousness raising, and the emphasis on sexual freedom and personal

151

autonomy alienated working-class women who were never drawn to the movement in large numbers. Other groups, such as lesbian feminists and black feminists, challenged the claims of the women's liberation movement to speak for all women and sought to bring their own experiences and priorities to the fore. Thus, in contrast to white middle-class women's criticism of the patriarchal nature of the family, black women were more likely to see the family as a source of strength and support against systematic racism. They were concerned that Reclaim the Night Marches and debates about rape reproduced stereotyped views of the sexualized black man who posed a threat to white women. Similarly, demands for legalized abortion failed to address issues such as forced sterilization that had a specific impact on black women. Black women found it difficult to accept that sexism was

---

BOX 6.3

bell hooks

bell hooks, a black American writer and social critic, was born Gloria Watkins in 1952 but took the name of her maternal great grandmother. She uses lower case for her name in order to put the emphasis on her writing. She is best known for her attacks on 'white supremacist capitalist patriarchy' which has involved a critique of the feminist movement for claiming to speak for all women when it represents white, middle-class perspectives. She argues that race, sex, class and sexual orientation are all inextricably linked and that social change requires them to be dealt with as a whole. Her most influential writings include *Ain't I a Woman? Black Women and Feminism* (1981); *Feminist Theory from Margin to Centre* (1984) and *Feminism is for Everybody: Passionate Politics* (2000). She also lectures throughout the world.

a more fundamental form of oppression than racism and sought to develop their own theories that would link gender and race. The American writer bell hooks has been particularly influential in challenging the racist assumptions of white feminism and in tracing black women's political and historical invisibility to the beginnings of slavery (hooks 1982).

Lesbian feminists argued that it was heterosexuality and not just male economic power that underpinned male supremacy. Authors such as Adrienne Rich and Mary Daly celebrated women's difference and argued that women could identify with each other in a variety of ways including the emotional as well as the political. For some activists, particularly in the United States, this implied the need for a separatist form of politics that would concentrate on women-identified concerns such as domestic violence. Some lesbians then suggested that heterosexual women could not be feminists since they collaborated with patriarchy and with men. This in turn led to acrimonious debates and splits in the movement in the late 1970s, in particular, over attitudes towards male violence, rape and pornography.

Divisions based on class, race, religion and ethnicity were just as common in the Third World as in Western societies. Community based working-class women's movements in Latin America, for example, tended to view feminist groups as middle class or as representing the interests of white women. In Asia feminists were conscious of the extent to which industrialized, wealthy countries in the region exploited women in less developed, neighbouring states and this contributed to the development of a complex feminist politics. Japanese women, for instance, linked their own oppression, in particular domestic violence, with the oppression of other women in South East Asia that resulted from

Japanese attempts to find cheap labour. As members of the Asian Women's Association Japanese feminists drew attention to the plight of women in the Philippines, Korea and Indonesia who were faced with either low pay in sweated industries or else work providing sexual services for tourists. They attempted to act in solidarity with Asian women rather than to see them as passive victims. In Islamic societies religious differences could lead to complex feminist alliances and strategies. In Iran, for example, the establishment of an Islamic republic in 1976 led to a loss of many rights that had been won over the course of the century. Nonetheless, Islamic feminists used their knowledge of the Koran to justify their arguments that women should have access to greater educational and employment opportunities. At the same time secular feminists reluctantly agreed to take up the veil as part of a bargaining strategy to enable them to make gains in employment, education and welfare.

The three International conferences held during the UN decade of women brought feminists together from different parts of the world, but they also revealed growing tensions between them. White, middle-class Western feminists were criticized for seeing their own goals and assumptions as universal ones. Muslim women, in particular, challenged the view that Islamic societies, with their emphasis on the patriarchal family, were repressive to women and that practices such as veiling were examples of women's lack of personal freedoms. Instead, they pointed to the ways in which Western feminists had been implicated in colonialism and suggested that their personal freedoms were illusory since women were used as sex objects in the media and in advertising. In contrast, Islamic feminists claimed that wearing the veil should be seen in a positive light, since it 'liberates them from the dictates of the fashion industry and the demands of the beauty myth' (Afshar 1996: 124).

Achievements of 'second wave' feminism

By the late 1970s it became far more difficult to contain differences between women and 'second wave feminism' appeared to have lost momentum. What had the movement achieved? It has been estimated that in western Europe at least a million women were activists and a further 12 million were sympathizers and supporters (Kaplan 1992: 17). In most countries the movement contributed towards legislation that aimed to enhance women's position, including equal pay, sex discrimination laws and, most important of all, the legalization of abortion. A key feature of 'second wave' feminism, however, was women's attempt to set up their own support networks outside mainstream political and social institutions. Women's health centres encouraged self-awareness about the female body and sexuality, while rape crisis centres provided practical help for women. In 1972 the first refuge in the world for battered women was established in Britain by Erin Pizzey .

Feminists showed that domestic violence and rape were not just the actions of violent individuals but were caused by social structures and expectations about male and female roles. In doing so they ensured that support would be forthcoming from state agencies in the future. Perhaps the most important aspect of the 1970s, however, was changing the terms in which the woman question was debated and in encouraging women to think differently about themselves and their place in the world. A new language had to be developed in order to make sense of the all-pervasive discrimination that women faced. It was argued that 'sexism' was embedded not just in the structures of institutions such as the workplace or the family, but also in the ways in which the roles of men and women, and the meaning of masculinity and femininity, were constructed in the media, in advertising and in everyday language. This ensured that the next generation of women would enter a very different world from the one that their mothers had struggled to change.

Further reading

Marlene Legates, *In Their Time. A History of Feminism in Western Society*, London: Routledge, 2001, Ch. 10 provides an overview of the origins of 'second wave' feminism. An analysis of the women's movement in individual countries in the 1950s and 60s can be found in: Claire Duchen and Irene Bandhauer Schöffmann (eds) *When the War Was Over: Women, War and Peace in Europe, 1940–1956*, London: Leicester University Press, 2000; Monica Threlfall (ed.) *Mapping the Women's Movement*, London: Verso, 1996; Gabriele Griffin and Rosi Braidotti (eds) *Thinking Differently. A Reader in European Women's Studies*, London: Zed Books, 2002; and Martin Pugh, *Women and the Women's Movement in Britain, 1914–1959*, Houndmills: Macmillan, 1992, Ch. 10.

The characteristics of 'second wave' feminism are discussed in: Drude Dahlerup (ed.) *The New Women's Movement*, London: Sage, 1986; Sheila Rowbotham, *The Past is Before Us. Feminism in Action since the 1960s*, London: Pandora, 1989; Françoise Picq, 'The History of the Feminist Movement in France', in Griffin and Braidotti (eds) *Thinking Differently* (above); and Ute Frevert, *Women in German History. From Bourgeois Emancipation to Sexual*

Liberation, Oxford: Berg, 1989. For a discussion of 'second wave' feminism in the context of left-wing politics in Europe, see Geoffrey Eley, *Forging Democracy. The History of the Left in Europe, 1850–2000*, Oxford: Oxford University Press, 2002.

Key texts of 'second wave' feminism include: Simone de Beauvoir, *The Second Sex*, London: Jonathan Cape, 1953 (Translation: H.M. Parshley); Betty Friedan, *The Feminine Mystique*, New York: W.W. Norton, 1963; Germaine Greer, *The Female Eunuch*, London: Paladin, 1971; Juliet Mitchell, *Woman's Estate*, Harmondsworth: Penguin, 1971; bel hooks, *Feminist Theory from Margin to Centre*, Boston: South End Press, 1984; and Kate Millett, *Sexual Politics*, New York: Doubleday, 1970.

For an overview of feminist theories in this period, see Imelda Whelehan, *Modern Feminist Thought. From the Second Wave to 'Post Feminism'*, Edinburgh: Edinburgh University Press, 1995; Gisela Kaplan, *Contemporary Western European Feminism*, London: UCL Press, 1992; and Jane Freedman, *Feminism*, Buckingham: Open University Press, 2001.

The attempts by feminists to integrate Marxism and feminism are explored in Heidi Hartmann, 'The Unhappy Marriage of Marxism and Feminism: Towards a More Progressive Union', in Lydia Sargent (ed.) *Women and Revolution*, London: Pluto, 1981. Marxist feminists differed over whether patriarchy was a useful tool of analysis, for example, see Judith Newton, Mary Ryan and Judith Walkowitz (eds) *Sex and Class in Women's History*, London: Routledge and Kegan Paul, 1983; and Sheila Rowbotham, 'The Trouble with Patriarchy', in Mary Evans (ed.) *The Women Question*, London: Fontana, 1982. For a discussion of the concept of patriarchy, see Sylvia Walby, *Theorizing Patriarchy*, Oxford: Blackwell, 1990. Mary Maynard provides a useful explanation of the 'three strands' of feminist thought and also gives a critique of these categories: 'Women's Studies' in Jackson and Jones (eds) *Contemporary Feminist Theories*, Edinburgh: Edinburgh University Press, 1998; and 'Beyond the "Big Three": The Development of Feminist Theory into the 1990s', *Women's History Review*, 4, 3, 1995. Jane Aaron and Sylvia Walby (eds) *Out of the Margins: Women's Studies in the Nineties*, London: Taylor and Francis, 1992 consider the extent to which, after two decades of scholarship, academic studies had been influenced by feminism.

Feminist theory and practice in Third World countries is discussed in: Chandra Talpade Mohanty, Ann Russo and Lourdes Torres (eds) *Third World Women and the Politics of Feminism*, Bloomington, IL: Indiana University Press, 1991; Haleh Afshar (ed.) *Women and Politics in the Third World*, London: Routledge, 1996; Leila Ahmed, *Women and Gender in Islam*, New Haven, CT: Yale University Press, 1992; Barbara J. Nelson and Najma Chowdhury (eds) *Women and Politics Worldwide*, New Haven, CT: Yale University Press, 1994; Jane S. Jaquette (ed.) *The Women's Movement in Latin America. Participation and Democracy*, Boulder, CO: Westview Press, 2nd edn 1994; Victoria E. Rodriguez, *Women's Participation in Mexican Political Life*, Boulder, CO: Westview Press, 1998; Rosalyn Terborg-Penn and Andrea Benton Rushing (eds) *Women in Africa and the African Diaspora*, Washington, DC: Harvard University Press, 1996, p. 18; Z.A. Mangaliso, 'Gender and Nation Building in South Africa', in Lois A. West (ed.) *Feminist Nationalisms*, London: Routledge, 1997; and Maxine Molyneux, 'Mobilisation without Emancipation? Women's Interest, the State and Revolution in Nicaragua', *Feminist Studies*, 11, 2, 1985.

CHAPTER 7

The twenty-first century – still making waves

WHAT HAS HAPPENED TO FEMINISM since the heady days of the women's liberation movement? Is there still a space for feminist politics in a world in which older political certainties appear to have collapsed with the fall of the Berlin Wall and the end of the Cold War? How should feminists deal with new political allegiances and conflicts – fundamentalist Islam against the corruption of the West, civil wars between ethnic groups or the increasing gap between rich and poor nations? As early as the 1980s 'second wave' feminists in Europe and North America could see that their movement was losing momentum and had become more fragmented. The slogan 'sisterhood is universal' was difficult to sustain when differences between women – including race, religion, ethnicity and sexual orientation – seemed more significant than their common interests as a sex.

New ways of thinking appeared to confirm this. Post-modernist theory, in particular, led feminists to question whether it was possible to speak of 'woman' as a distinct category. In her influential book, *Am I That Name?*, Denise Riley suggested that ' "woman" is historically, discursively constructed and always relatively to other categories which themselves change' (Riley 1988 in Hall 1991: 205). If the individual self is fragmented and likely to have multiple identities that change over time, it would be difficult to find a straightforward link between experience and political activity or to conceive of a politics based on collective interests as a sex – both of which had been crucial for 'second wave' feminism.

Women also still took action outside formal political and professional structures. They organized self-help groups at a local level, took part in campaigns over specific issues, such as child-care facilities and tried to get their message across by forming publishing collectives, theatre groups or organizing other cultural activities. There were moments when women could be mobilized in larger numbers. In Britain, for example, a women-only peace camp was set up at the Greenham Common nuclear base in 1981. In the following year over 30,000 women encircled the base and left personal items such as photographs or children's clothes tied to the fence. This provides a good example of how informal networks could be effective in leading to the organization of a large-scale protest. Similarly in the United States, three quarters of a million women were still prepared to march on Washington in 1992 when abortion rights were under threat. Women might join together in specific identity groups, or in single-issue protests, but this seemed like a far cry from the mass mobilization to challenge a common oppression that had characterized the earlier women's liberation movement.

A hostile political climate also made it difficult for a women's movement to flourish. A move to the right in politics led to a new emphasis on the importance of the traditional family and to attacks on some of the gains made by women, in particular, abortion rights. This 'backlash' against 'second wave' feminism was then reinforced by the popular media which used the term post-feminism – not to describe something that occurred after feminism, but to imply that there was an active rejection of 'second wave feminism' and its outmoded ideas. Younger women were encouraged to exercise personal choice, in particular, as consumers of clothes and beauty products, and to react against the stereotype of the serious feminist who wore dungarees, used little make up and was anti-male. This attack on feminism can be seen as a defensive reaction of a male establishment against the threat of change that 'second wave feminism' had posed. On the other hand, there were also feminist authors who criticized second wave feminism, in particular, for its preoccupation with rape and sexual harassment that implied women were victims. The most well known of these authors – who was taken up extensively by the media – was Naomi Wolf, the author of *The Beauty Myth* (1991) and *Fire Within Fire* (1993). Although she argued that the media were largely responsible for creating a negative image of feminism, she also blamed the movement itself for being too rigid in its definitions and for holding back women from doing whatever they wanted.

Post-feminism was used to imply that there was no longer a need for feminism now that women had made so many gains in legal, economic, political and reproductive rights. Indeed, throughout the world girls and women took full advantage of an increase in educational and employment opportunities and began to make inroads into positions of power in many organizations. Feminism as an approach and a category of analysis became more embedded in academic subjects and women were able to gain positions of influence in higher education and in the media. Publishing houses and journals established by women then provided an important outlet for feminist scholarship. Women were also able to make their voices heard within formal political structures both at a national level and internationally, in the European Union and the United Nations. In 1995, for example, the UN sponsored a World Conference on Women in Beijing. Working through political parties, trade unions and the professions feminists attempted to influence policies affecting the lives of women, in particular in the area of social welfare. In Ireland, for instance, women took an active part in the referenda in the 1980s on abortion and the removal of the constitutional ban on divorce. Women did not necessarily use their positions of power and influence within organizations, however, to challenge gender inequalities. They were more likely to press for social welfare reforms to improve women's health or their housing conditions rather than to focus on empowering women to take control over their lives. The subversive, questioning side of feminism, therefore, appeared to be lost.

Not all women benefited from the social and economic changes of the last two decades of the twentieth century. In the year 2000 women, who were just over half of the world's population, still performed two thirds of the world's work hours, earned less than one tenth of its income and owned less than 1% of its property. Of the estimated 1.3 billion people living in poverty, over 70% were female and there were still vast differences in the maternal mortality rates and general health statistics between sub-Saharan Africa, East Asia and industrialized countries. Even in the West there were paradoxes (Billson and Fluehr-Lobban 2005: 5–6). Young women were told that they had 'never had it so good' and were doing well in education and in employment. But violence against women, exploitative advertising, pornography and prostitution were still endemic. The World Health Organization, for instance, estimated in 2000 that one in five women globally had been physically or sexually abused at some time in her life. The freedom to express sexual desire and to have relationships outside marriage without a social stigma were positive developments for young women, but were accompanied by a greater risk of sexually transmitted diseases and a greater respectability for pornography in the public sphere.

Changes that might on the surface have brought benefits for women could prove to be contradictory in their effects. Without the context of a strong women's movement, for instance, it was difficult to frame reforms in feminist terms. Thus, professional women who sought improvements in social welfare services such as reproductive rights emphasized health and the well-being of families rather than women's right to choose and sexual autonomy. Similarly, the introduction of democratic governments could, paradoxically, marginalize women's needs and feminist demands. In Latin America, for example, political parties took up feminist demands around employment and social welfare, but were reluctant to pursue reproductive rights, sexuality and domestic violence. Women became less significant as political actors, their activities were more diffuse and there was little sense that the reforms introduced were designed to challenge male power. In eastern Europe, democratization in the 1980s opened up a space for women to organize together, but the new, male-dominated parliaments increasingly questioned the reproductive rights women had enjoyed under socialism.

In this context, as a new millennium approached, there were signs of a new vitality in feminist politics. Collective actions by women and debates about the future of feminism raised the possibility that we were entering a period of 'third wave feminism' in the twenty-first century. This suggests that for a new generation of women, as well as for many older campaigners, feminism still has a place in their lives and certainly is neither dead nor irrelevant. Throughout the history of feminism there has always been debate about what it means to be a feminist, which goals should be pursued and which tactics should be used. Feminism in the twenty-first century is no exception. It simply has to deal with different patterns, priorities and contradictions which are going to affect the ways in which women act politically.

There have been numerous disagreements about the meaning of 'third wave feminism', and indeed whether there is something distinctive that can be assigned that label. But all participants in the debate contest the view that we are living in a post-feminist age. It is surely significant that Germaine Greer, author of *The Female Eunuch*, a key text of the women's liberation movement once again came to the fore in 1999 with another book *The Whole Woman*. In this she argued that post-feminism had encouraged women to think they could have it all – a career, motherhood, beauty and a good sex life. Their role as consumers and the importance of personal lifestyle choices had been emphasized at the expense of politics. And yet, as she pointed out, this applied largely to the affluent West where 'the exercising of one person's freedom may be directly linked to another's oppression'. Thus, a collapse in economic power of the majority of women in the world has been a direct consequence of Western power and control. In this situation, she asked, how could a woman believe that she has passed beyond feminism (Gamble 2001: 51)?

If feminism is still alive and well in the twenty-first century, what does it aim to do and does it have a different character from the feminisms that have gone before? Generation is a key issue. Young women who have benefited from social changes since 'second wave feminism' focus on the body and sexuality as areas where struggle still has to take place. They have also joined into campaigns around global issues including environmentalism, anti-capitalist and anti-corporate activities, cultural production and human-rights questions. They perceive these as women's issues but do not see them in isolation from human issues – a perspective that would have been familiar to peace and human rights campaigners in the inter-war years.

Feminists active in the women's liberation movement of the 1970s have also attempted to develop different strategies for the new millennium. Elaine Showalter, for example, an American author and feminist campaigner suggests community activists, seeking to improve women's lives through better child-care or health facilities, should use the political and economic power that women now hold to help their cause. Debates around the best strategies to follow are not new and echo concerns that feminists have expressed from the mid-nineteenth century onwards. Should women organize together in women only groups, both as the most effective way to make an impact and also because this provides a safe environment in which consciousness of what it means to be a woman can be raised? Or is it better, in a mixed-sex world, to work with men in organizations addressing common concerns? Should women work through formal structures to achieve change or does this dilute the whole meaning of feminism with its emphasis on non-hierarchical ways of acting together and informal networks of support?

What has emerged from these debates is the importance of developing a variety of strategies for achieving change; women in parliaments throughout the world are likely to be more effective in raising feminist issues if they have the support of an autonomous women's group outside. Involvement in community struggles over child care, school closures or health facilities, which do not at first appear to have a feminist agenda, can lead to links being made between local activists and feminist groups. Moreover, whether structures are formal or informal collective campaigns lead to networks of support being developed at all levels. In a new political context, and with the distance that enables feminists to re-appraise 'second wave feminism', many issues can be approached in far more complex ways than in the past. Instead of using the slogan a 'woman's right to choose', campaigners around reproductive rights are likely to look at the language of rights that has framed the debates and to consider compromises that might need to be made to ensure legislative success.

'Third wave' feminism might be difficult to define – and indeed the label may have very little meaning. But debates around this issue show that feminism still has vitality and that it is possible for women to take common action for political purposes and not just for individual, personal fulfilment. Women have found, and continue to find, a variety of spaces in which to operate and have expressed greater optimism that both identity politics and single-issue campaigns can be a springboard for broader actions. In France, for example, debate over the small number of women elected to representative institutions has reinvigorated the women's movement and brought a new visibility to feminist politics. Third World feminists, in particular, have argued that it is possible to conceive of a different type of universal feminism that is no longer rooted within the norms and perspectives of white, Western feminists. They suggest that if emphasis is placed on the great variety of feminisms and on an understanding of the specific contexts in which women develop their strategies and their priorities, feminists would be able more easily to speak to each other across national and cultural barriers. In many instances, such as the women of Burundi who have organized committees to bring together villagers engaged in ethnic disputes, there is an attempt to find common ground as women despite differences.

Feminism has never been a monolithic movement. There have always been many feminisms united by the fact that at their heart they recognize men's power over women and seek to challenge women's subordination. Feminism is not necessarily synonymous with a highly organized and visible women's movement that explicitly challenges gender inequalities and seeks to 'turn the world upside down'. This is not likely to happen very often. As Showalter notes, 'movements by their nature are infrequent and localised events' with a 'specific and attainable goal' (Gillis, Howie and Munford 2004: 60). The absence of a well organized and seemingly united women's movement, however, does not mean a corresponding absence of feminist activity. In the twenty-first century there are still 'persistent, patterned inequalities' (Jackson and Jones 1998: 10) between men and women throughout the world. This makes it imperative not to lose sight of the category 'woman' and to continue to expose the unequal power relationship between the sexes. It is likely that women will find many different sites, as they have done in the past, in which to make their voices heard and to put forward their demands. Debates will continue about how best to develop a 'feminist consciousness', about the aims and objectives to be pursued and about whether to organize in single or in mixed-sex groups. The many differences between women are bound to lead to a variety of feminisms, but this does not have to prevent women from working collectively. Political and economic globalization are increasingly linking women together across national boundaries and raise the possibility of joint actions in the future against common forms of oppression. As one author notes, in a recent collection of essays on 'third wave' feminism: 'never mind which number we're on, we need to be making waves' (Spencer 2004: 12).

Further reading

Key texts exploring the implications of post-modernism for feminist theory and practice are: Denise Riley, *Am I That Name? Feminism and the Category of 'Women' in History*, London: Macmillan, 1988; and Joan Scott, *Gender and the Politics of History*, New York: Columbia University Press, 1988. The implications of their work for feminist history is discussed in June Purvis, 'From "Women Worthies" to Post-Structuralism? Debate and Controversy in Women's History in Britain', in June Purvis (ed.) *Women's History. Britain, 1850–1945*, London: UCL Press, 1995. The 'backlash' against feminism in the late 1980s and 1990s is discussed in: F. Rush, 'The Many Faces of Backlash', in Dorchen E.H. Lendholt and Janice G. Raymond (eds) *The Sexual Liberals and the Attack* on *Feminism*, Oxford: Pergamon Press, 1990; and Susan Faludi, *Backlash: The Undeclared War Against Women*, London: Chatto and Windus, 1991. Two stimulating but controversial feminist texts in the 1990s were: Naomi Wolf, *The Beauty Myth: How Images of Beauty Are Used Against Women*, New York: Vintage, 1991; and Germaine Greer, *The Whole Woman*, London: Doubleday, 1999.

For a discussion of the continuing vitality of feminism in the 1990s and beyond, see Gabriele Griffin (ed.) *Feminist Activism in the 1990s*, London: Taylor and Francis, 1995; Breda Gray and Louise Ryan, 'The Politics of Irish Identity and the Interconnections between Feminism, Nationhood and Colonialism', in Ruth Roach Pierson and Nupur Chaudhuri (eds) *Nation, Empire, Colony: Historicizing Gender and Race*, Bloomington, IN: Indiana University Press, 1998; Vera Mackie, 'Feminist Critiques of Modern Japanese Politics', in M. Threlfall (ed.) *Mapping the Women's Movement*, London: Verso; Sara Mills, 'Post-Colonial Feminist Theory' and Stevi Jackson and Jackie Jones, 'Thinking for Ourselves: An Introduction to Feminist Theorising', in S. Jackson and J. Jones (eds) *Contemporary Feminist Theories*, Edinburgh: Edinburgh University Press, 1998.

Global dimensions of feminism are considered in: Amrita Basu (ed.) *The Challenge of Local Feminisms*, Oxford: Westview Press, 1995. Information on women's lives world-wide can be found in Janet Mancini Billson and Carolyn Fluehr-Lobban (eds) *Female Well-Being. Toward a Global Theory of Social Change*, London: Zed Books, 2005.

For an overview of contemporary feminist debates, see Valerie Bryson, *Feminist Debaes; Issues of Theory and Political Practice*,

Houndmills: Macmillan, 1999; Sarah Gamble (ed.) *Feminism and Postfeminism*, London: Routledge, 2001; Stacy Gillis, Gillian Howie and Rebecca Munford (eds) *Third Wave Feminism: A Critical Exploration*, Houndmills: Palgrave Macmillan, 2004.

References

Afshar, H. (ed.) (1996) *Women and Politics in the Third World*. London: Routledge.

Ahmed, L. (1992) *Women and Gender in Islam*. New Haven, CT: Yale University Press.

Alberti, J. (1989) *Beyond Suffrage: Feminists in War and Peace, 1914–28*. Houndmills: Macmillan.

Alvarez, S.E. (1994) 'The (trans)formation of feminism(s) and gender politics in democratizing Brazil', in Jaquette, J.S. (ed.) *The Women's Movement in Latin America. Participation and Democracy*. Boulder, CO: Westview Press, pp. 13–63.

Badran, M. (1995) *Feminists, Islam and Nation: Gender and the Making of Modern Egypt*. Princeton, NJ: Princeton University Press.

Banks, O. (1980) *Faces of Feminism*. Oxford: Martin Robertson.

Basu, A. (ed.) (1995) *The Challenge of Local Feminisms: Women's Movements in Global Perspective*. Oxford: Westview Press.

Beaumont, C. (2000) 'Citizens not feminists: the boundary negotiated between citizenship and feminism by mainstream women's organisations in England, 1928–39', *Women's History Review*, 9, 2, pp. 411–29.

Billson, J.M. and **Fluehr-Lobban, C.** (eds) (2005) *Female Well-Being. Toward a Global Theory of Social Change*. London: Zed Books.

Blom, I. (1980) 'The struggle for women's suffrage in Norway, 1885–1913', *Scandinavian Journal of History*, 5, 3, pp. 3–22.

Blom, I. (1998) Conference report, Gendered Nations: Nationalisms and Gender Order in the Long Nineteenth Century – International Comparisons, www.h-netmsu.edu/~women/threads/report-nation.html

Bosch, M. with Kloosterman, A. (eds) (1990) *Politics and Friendship: Letters from the International Woman Suffrage Alliance, 1902–1942*. Columbus, OH: Columbus University Press.

Bosch, M. (1999) 'Colonial dimensions of Dutch women's suffrage: Aletta Jacobs's travel letters from Africa and Asia, 1911–12', *Journal of Women's History*, 11, 2, pp. 199–220.

Brenner, J. (1996) 'The best of times, the worst of times. Feminism in the United States', in M. Threlfall (ed.) *Mapping the Women's Movement*. London: Verso, pp. 7–72.

Bryson, V. (1999) *Feminist Debates: Issues of Theory and Political Practice*. Houndmills: Macmillan.

Burton, A. (1994) *Burdens of History: British Feminists, Indian Women and Imperial Culture, 1865–1914*, Chapel Hill, NC: University of North Carolina Press.

Burton, A. (2002) ' "States of injury": Josephine Butler on slavery, citizenship, and the Boer War', in Fletcher, I.C., Mayhall, L.E.N. and Levine, P. (eds) *Women's Suffrage in the British Empire: Citizenship, Nation and Race*. London: Routledge, pp. 338–61.

Bush, J. (2002) 'British women's anti-suffragism and the forward policy, 1908–14', *Women's History Review*, 11, 3, pp. 431–54.

Caine, B. (1992) *Victorian Feminists*. Oxford: Oxford University Press.

Caine, B. (1997) *English Feminism, 1780–1980*. Oxford: Oxford University Press.

De Beauvoir, S. (1953) *The Second Sex*. London: Jonathan Cape.

Edmondson, L.H. (1992) *Women and Society in Russia and the Soviet Union*. Cambridge: Cambridge University Press.

Ehrick, C. (1998) ' "Madrinas and missionaries": Uruguay and the pan-American women's movement', *Gender and History*, 10, 3, pp. 406–24.

Eley, G. (2002) *Forging Democracy. The History of the Left in Europe, 1850–2000*. Oxford: Oxford University Press.

Evans, R.J. (1977) *The Feminists: Women's Emancipation Movements in Europe, America and Australasia, 1840–1920*. London: Croom Helm.

Friedan, B. (1963) *The Feminine Mystique*. New York: Dell.

Gadant, M. (1995) *Le Nationalism Algérien et les Femmes*. Paris: Editions l'Harmattan.

Gamble, S. (ed.) (2001) *Feminism and Postfeminism*. London: Routledge.

Gerhard, U. (2002) 'The women's movement in Germany', in Griffin, G. and Braidotti, R. (eds) *Thinking Differently. A Reader in European Women's Studies*. London: Zed Books, pp. 321–31.

Gillis, S., Howie, G. and **Munford, R.** (eds) (2004) *Third Wave Feminism: A Critical Exploration*. Houndmills: Palgrave Macmillan.

Gleadle, K. (2001) 'British women and radical politics in the Late Nonconformist Enlightenment, c. 1780–1830', in Vickery, A. (ed.) *Women, Privilege and Power. British Politics, 1750 to the Present*. Stanford, CA: Stanford University Press, pp. 123–51.

Gleadle, K. and **Richardson, S.** (eds) (2000) *Women in British Politics, 1760–1860. The Power of the Petticoat*. Basingstoke: Macmillan.

Gray, B. and **Ryan, L.** (1998) 'The politics of Irish identity and the interconnections between feminism, nationhood and colonialism', in Pierson, R.R. and Chaudhuri, N. (eds) *Nation, Empire, Colony: Historicizing Gender and Race*. Bloomington, IN: Indiana University Press, pp. 121–38.

Greer, G. (1971) *The Female Eunuch*. London: Paladin.

Greer, G. (1999) *The Whole Woman*. London: Doubleday.

Grimshaw, P. (1987) *Women's Suffrage in New Zealand*. Auckland: University of Auckland Press.

Hagemann, G. (2002) 'Citizenship and social order: gender politics in twentieth century Norway and Sweden', *Women's History Review*, 11, 3, pp. 417–29.

Hagemann, K. and **Hall, C.** (eds) *Gendered Nations: Nationalism and Gender Order in the Long Nineteenth Century*. Oxford: Berg, pp. 159–76.

Hall, C. (1991) 'Politics, post-structuralism and feminist history', *Gender and History*, 3, 2, pp. 204–10.

Hannam, J. and **Hunt, K.** (2001) *Socialist Women: Britain 1880s–1920s*. London: Routledge.

Hause, S.C. with **Kenney, A.R.** (1984) *Women's Suffrage and Social Politics in the French Third Republic*. Princeton, NJ: Princeton University Press.

Holton, S.S. (1996) *Suffrage Days: Stories from the Women's Suffrage Movement*. London: Routledge.

hooks, b. (1982) *Ain't I a Woman*. London: Pluto.

hooks, b. (1984) *Feminist Theory from Margin to Centre*. Boston, MA: South End Press.

Hunt, K. (1996) *Equivocal Feminists. The Social Democratic Federation and the Woman Question, 1884–1911*. Cambridge: Cambridge University Press.

Jackson, S. and **Jones, J.** (1998) 'Thinking for ourselves: an introduction to feminist theorising', in Jackson, S. and Jones, J. (eds) *Contemporary Feminist Theories*. Edinburgh: Edinburgh University Press, pp. 1–10.

Jacquette, J.S. (ed.) (1994) *The Women's Movement in Latin America: Participation and Democracy*. Boulder, CO: Westview Press.

Jayawardena, K. (1986) *Feminism and Nationalism in the Third World*, London: Zed Books.

Kaplan, G. (1992) *Contemporary Western European Feminism*. London: UCL.

Kean, H. (1994) 'Searching for the present in past defeat: the construction of historical and political identity in British feminism in the 1920s and 30s', *Women's History Review*, 3, 1, pp. 57–80.

Kent, S.K. (1990) *Sex and Suffrage in Britain, 1860–1914*. London: Routledge.

Kent, S.K. (1993) *Making Peace: The Reconstruction of Gender in Inter-War Britain*. Princeton, NJ: Princeton University Press.

Lake, M. (2000) 'The ambiguities for feminists of national belonging: race and gender in the imagined Australian community', in Blom, I., Hagemann, K. and Hall, C. (eds) *Gendered Nations: Nationalism and Gender Order in the Long Nineteenth Century*. Oxford: Berg, pp. 159–76.

Lavrin, A. (1995) *Women, Feminism and Social Change in Argentina, Chile and Uruguay, 1890–1940*. Lincoln: University of Nebraska Press.

Legates, M. (2001) *In Their Time. A History of Feminism in Western Society*. London: Routledge.

Lerner, G. (1979) *The Majority Finds Its Past: Placing Women in History*. Oxford: Oxford University Press.

Levine, P. (1990) 'Love, feminism and friendship in later nineteenth-century England', *Women's Studies International Forum*, 13, 1/2, pp. 63–78.

Liddington, J. and **Norris, J.** (1978) *One Hand Tied Behind Us. The Rise of the Women's Suffrage Movement*. London: Virago.

McMillan, J.F. (2000) *France and Women, 1789–1914. Gender, Society and Politics*. London: Routledge.

Mayhall, L.E.N. (2003) *The Militant Suffrage Movement: Citizenship and Resistance in Britain, 1860–1930*. Oxford: Oxford University Press.

Maynard, M. (1998) 'Women's studies', in Jackson, S. and Jones, J. (eds) *Contemporary Feminist Theories*. Edinburgh: Edinburgh University Press, pp. 247–59.

Midgley, C. (1992) *Women Against Slavery: The British Campaigns, 1780–1870*. London: Routledge.

Midgley, C. (2001) 'British women, women's rights and empire, 1790–1850', in Grimshaw, P., Holmes, K. and Lake, M. (eds) *Women's Rights and Human Rights*. Basingstoke: Palgrave, pp. 3–15.

Mill, J.S. (1869; 1985) *On the Subjection of Women*. London: Dent.

Millett, K. (1969) *Sexual Politics*. London: Rupert Hart-Davis.

Mitchell, J. (1971) *Woman's Estate*. Harmondsworth: Penguin.

Offen, K. (2000) *European Feminisms, 1700–1950: A Political History*. Stanford, CA: Stanford University Press.

Outram, D. (1995) *The Enlightenment*. Cambridge: Cambridge University Press.

Pateman, C. (1992) 'Equality, difference and subordination: the politics of motherhood and women's citizenship', in Bock, G. and James, S. (eds) *Beyond Equality and Difference: Citizenship, Feminist Politics and Female Subjectivity*. London: Routledge, pp. 17–31.

Phillip, T. (1978) 'Feminism and nationalist politics in Egypt', in Beck, L. and Keddie, N. (eds) *Women in the Muslim World*. Cambridge, MA: Harvard University Press, pp. 277–94.

Picq, F. (2002) 'The history of the feminist movement in France', in Griffin, G. and Braidotti, R. (eds) *Thinking Differently. A Reader in European Women's Studies*. London: Zed Books, pp. 313–20.

Rendall, J. (1985) *The Origins of Modern Feminism: Women in Britain, France and the United States, 1780–1860*. Basingstoke: Macmillan.

Rendall, J. (1994) 'Citizenship, Culture and Civilisation: The Languages of British Suffragists, 1866–1874', in Daley, C. and Nolan, M. (eds) *Suffrage and Beyond*. Auckland: Auckland University Press, pp. 127–50.

Rendall, J. (2001) 'John Stuart Mill, liberal politics and the movements for women's suffrage, 1865–1973', in Vickery, A. (ed.) *Women, Privilege and Power. British Politics, 1750 to the Present*. Stanford, CA: Stanford University Press, pp. 000–000.

Riley, D. (1988) *Am I That Name? Feminism and the 'Category' of Women in History*. London: Macmillan.

Rowbotham, S. (1973) *Hidden from History. 300 Years of Women's Oppression and the Fight Against It*. London: Pluto.

Rowbotham, S. (1989) *The Past is Before Us. Feminism in Action since the 1960s*. London: Pandora.

Rupp, L. (1997) *Worlds of Women: The Making of an International Women's Movement*. Princeton, NJ: Princeton University Press.

Scully, P. (2000) 'White maternity and black infancy: the rhetoric of race in the South African women's suffrage movement, 1890–1930', in Fletcher, I.C., Mayhall, L.E.N. and Levine, P. (eds) *Women's Suffrage in the British Empire: Citizenship, Nation and Race*. London: Routledge, pp. 68–83.

Sinha, M. (2000) 'Suffragism and internationalism. The enfranchisement of British and Indian women under an imperial state', in Fletcher, I.C., Mayhall, L.E.N. and Levine, P. (eds) *Women's Suffrage in the British Empire: Citizenship, Nation and Race*. London: Routledge, pp. 224–39.

Sinha, M., Guy, D.J. and **Woollacott, A.** (1998) 'Introduction: why feminisms and internationalism?', *Gender and History*, 10, 3, p. 345.

Smith, H.L. (ed.) (1990) *British Feminism in the Twentieth Century*. Aldershot: Edward Elgar.

Sowerwine, S. (1987) 'The socialist women's movement from 1850–1940', in Bridenthal, R., Koontz, C. and Stuard, S. (eds) *Becoming Visible: Women in European History*. Boston, MA: Houghton Mifflin, pp. 399–428.

Spencer, J. (2004) 'Introduction: genealogies', in Cullis, S., Howie, G. and Munford, R. (eds) *Third Wave Feminism: A Critical Exploration*. Houndmills: Palgrave Macmillan, pp. 142–53.

Steady, F.C. (1996) 'African feminism: a worldwide perspective', in Terborg-Penn, R. and Rushing, A.B. (eds) *Women in Africa and the African Diaspora*. Washington, DC: Harvard University Press, pp. 3–21.

Summers, A. (2000) *Female Lives, Moral States*. Newbury: Threshold Press.

Taylor, B. (1983) *Eve and the New Jerusalem. Socialism and Feminism in the Nineteenth Century*. London: Virago.

Thane, P. (1993) 'Women in the British Labour Party and the construction of state welfare', in Koven, S. and Michel, S. (eds) *Mothers of a New World: Maternalist Politics and the Origins of the Welfare States*. Routledge: London, pp. 343–77.

Thane, P. (2001) 'What difference did the vote make?', in Vickery, A. (ed.) *Women, Privilege and Power. British Politics 1750 to the Present.* Stanford, CA: Stanford University Press, pp. 253–88.

Thompson, E. (2000) *Colonial Citizens. Republican Rights, Paternal Privilege and Gender in French Syria and Lebanon.* New York: Columbia University Press.

Tickner, L. (1987) *The Spectacle of Women: Imagery of the Suffrage Campaign, 1907–1914.* London: Chatto and Windus.

Ward, M. (1993) ' "Suffrage first – above all else!" An account of the Irish suffrage movement', in Smyth, A. (ed.) *Irish Women's Studies Reader.* Dublin: Attic Press, pp. 20–44.

Ware, V. (1992) *Beyond The Pale. White Women, Racism and History.* London: Verso.

Whelehan, I. (1995) *Modern Feminist Thought. From the Second Wave to 'Post Feminism'.* Edinburgh: Edinburgh University Press.

Wolf, N. (1991) *The Beauty Myth: How Images of Beauty are Used Against Women.* New York: Vintage.

Wolf, N. (1993) *Fire Within Fire: New Female Power and How it will Change the Twenty-First Century.* Toronto, Ontario: Random House.

Wollstonecraft, M. (1792; 1993) *A Vindication of the Rights of Woman.* Harmondsworth: Penguin.

Woollacott, A. (1998) 'Inventing Commonwealth and pan-Pacific feminisms: Australian women's internationalist activism in the 1920s–30s', *Gender and History*, 10, 3, pp. 381–405.

Yeo, E.J. (ed.) (1997) *Mary Wollstonecraft and 200 Years of Feminisms.* London: Rivers Oram.

Index

of aboriginal women from the franchise. Only a few suffragists, including Rose Scott, protested at this exclusion and sought to protect and encourage the culture of Aboriginal women. Similarly in South Africa suffragists rarely alluded to issues of race except when the 'native question' dominated national politics. When they did so they argued that women as mothers were uniquely qualified to legislate on issues affecting the black population who were akin to children. Thus, they appealed for the vote in ways that could 'reinforce both gendered stereotypes of women's capacities as well as entrenched ideas in the white communities about the supposed political immaturity of black South Africans' (Scully 2000: 68). For the most part, suffragists avoided race by demanding votes for women on the same terms as men, but they had little difficulty in accepting the exclusion of Cape Africans, defined as people of mixed descent, from voting rolls in the 1920s.

Widening the basis of support after 1900

Women had made little headway by the end of the nineteenth century in their campaign to have a voice in national politics. They had gained the vote in New Zealand (1893) and Australia (1902), where the suffrage movement was smaller and more moderate than in Britain and the United States. Elsewhere voting rights were confined to local politics where it was thought that women would bring the skills of good housekeeping to the running of local services. In Sweden and Britain, for example, single women who fulfilled the property qualifications were able to vote for municipal councils in 1862 and 1869 respectively, while in the United States women were able to vote at a state level by the 1890s in Wyoming, Utah, Colorado and Idaho.

A new sense of excitement was generated by the suffrage campaign, however, after the turn of the century. Recently formed organizations attracted a broadly based membership and began to develop different methods and political strategies. This meant that the demand for women's suffrage had a far greater impact on national politics than ever before. In the United States the National American Woman Suffrage Association, formed from a merger of existing groups in 1890, expanded its membership and made greater efforts to involve black and working-class

---

BOX 3.3

National American Woman Suffrage Association (NAWSA)

The National Woman Suffrage Association and the American Woman Suffrage Association, that had split over 20 years before, came together in 1890 to form the NAWSA. The first two presidents, Elizabeth Cady Stanton (1890–2) and Susan B. Anthony (1892–1900) had a great deal of experience but there was no agreement among the leaders about the best tactics to use and little direction was given to state campaigns. Dr Anna Shaw, president from 1904 to 1915, was an inspiring speaker and membership rose from 17,000 to 200,000, but it was not until Carrie Chapman Catt served her second term as president from 1915 that a consistent strategy for achieving the vote was developed. This entailed concentrating on a federal amendment, attempting to persuade President Wilson to give his support and mobilizing support from state suffrage groups. The painstaking organization, lobbying and petitioning of NAWSA at state and national levels played an important part in ensuring that enough votes were cast, in particular in the Senate, to ratify the Nineteenth Amendment in 1920 that gave women the vote.